Decoding the Workplace

Decoding the Workplace

50 Keys to Understanding People in Organizations

John Ballard, PhD

PRAEGER™

An Imprint of ABC-CLIO, LLC

Santa Barbara, California • Denver, Colorado

Library of Congress Cataloging-in-Publication Data
Ballard, John (Professor)
    Decoding the workplace : 50 keys to understanding people in organizations / John
Ballard, PhD.
        pages cm
Includes bibliographical references and index.
    ISBN 978-1-4408-3826-2 (alk. paper) – ISBN 978-1-4408-3827-9 (ebook)
    1. Organizational behavior.   2. Corporate culture.   3. Psychology, Industrial.
    I. Title.
    HD58.7.B353 2015
    302.3′5–dc23   2015001793

ISBN: 978-1-4408-3826-2
EISBN: 978-1-4408-3827-9

19 18 17 16 15   1 2 3 4 5

This book is also available on the World Wide Web as an eBook.
Visit www.abc-clio.com for details.

Praeger
An Imprint of ABC-CLIO, LLC

ABC-CLIO, LLC
130 Cremona Drive, P.O. Box 1911
Santa Barbara, California 93116-1911

This book is printed on acid-free paper ∞

Manufactured in the United States of America

To
My darling Emily, my wife,
who grounds my life
and makes all things possible
And to our grandchildren
Justine, Jackson, Allison, Calvin
whom we deeply love and cherish

Contents

Preface

It was the grand opening of a business in a new and bigger location. The owner was very successful. He had significantly grown his business. Tonight was a special night for regular customers and old friends. Shortly after I arrived, the owner noticed me and motioned for me to join him.

"Good evening," I said, "Very impressive. You have done well."

Without blinking an eye, he replied, "I could not have done it without you. In many ways you are a big part of my success."

Greatly surprised, I muttered, "Not really. Surely not. You have done this." He raised his hand and stopped me.

"But you taught me lots of little things that have made all the difference—how to think about what I do, how to understand people, how to treat my employees. No, I would not be here tonight but for the good advice you have shared across the years."

I thanked him and moved along.

In this book is much of that advice.

Would you like:

- a better understanding of the workplace around you;
- a better understanding of others;
- a better understanding of yourself;
- ideas to improve your effectiveness; and
- ideas to improve your decision making in the daily business of the workplace?

Or perhaps you know someone who would. I offer no guarantees, but my experience is that there are insights in these pages that will benefit many people.

I am a university professor who teaches management and behavior in organizations. I am also a former manager and consultant with decades of practical experience. For many years, students in my courses—especially the graduate students who were managers in the "real world"—have suggested that I write a book, a book that would capture what we discuss in class. Such were the origins of this volume.

I have been studying management for a lifetime. I know the scholarly literature on leading, managing, and behavior in the workplace. I also know the school of hard knocks, and how ideas are translated or fail to be translated. Management books for the masses tend to be written mostly by successful business people and consultants. With some notable exceptions, such as Rosabeth Moss Kanter and John Kotter, most professors are more likely to write for other business professors. Too frequently academic books by professors are hard to read and difficult to apply to the "real world." Conversely, some management trade books would benefit from a firmer foundation in the scientific research on what we know about people, leading, and managing. Stephen Robbins wrote in *The Truth About Managing People*, "Much of it [management advice from these books] . . . is a gross generalization, ambiguous, inconsistent, or superficial. Some of it is even downright wrong."[1]

My favorite management philosopher lived over 100 years ago. In the 1920s Mary Follett, often called "the prophet of management," wrote that stories and examples are essential to learning how to lead and understand others. I totally agree. I find that stories and anecdotes derived from organizational life clarify concepts and make the concepts easier to remember.

To illustrate the concepts and ideas in the chapters that follow, I have shared from my work and life experiences. I also have used short stories or vignettes—creations and composites from life in the workplace. Any similarities to specific people or organizations are unintentional. Because most of these examples represent common organizational experiences, you could find them very similar to situations with which you are familiar. You might say to yourself, "I've seen that" or "something like that happened just the other week." Reflecting on your own experiences will move you closer to decoding your workplace.

As college and university professors, we are taught to focus on detailed research studies published in scholarly journals. We question the limits to which we can apply the results of our studies to other situations. We sort through results of research studies to validate theories. To some academicians my presentation of theory and research at times could seem overly simplified. To echo Douglas McGregor, professor and author of the 1960s' best-selling management book, *The Human Side of Enterprise*:

> If all of the qualifications which would be required by a truly adequate treatment were introduced, the gross essentials which are particularly significant

for management would be obscured. These generalizations do not misrepresent the facts, but they do ignore some complexities of human behavior which are relatively unimportant for our purpose.[2]

Human behavior is very complex. This book focuses on essentials to help you understand the workplace, the concepts I consider to be essential to understanding yourself and others. I present them from my perspective, as seen through my lens—as a management scholar and as a manager and consultant. This book is not a primer on management or organizational behavior per se. There are many excellent academic books that do that. My objective is to put concepts from the management and organizational behavior literature in easy-to-understand terms and illustrate using stories and examples. In this book are meaningful ideas that can help readers decode the workplace and navigate their work lives. My hope is that somewhere in these pages you will find some idea, some concept, some insight that will make your life a little better.

Part I: First Thoughts

CHAPTER ONE

Using Keys to Decode the Workplace

Laura had only been in her new job a few weeks. It was her first "real" job, the first since she graduated from college. She was very glad to be employed. Her entry-level position was in a nice office setting. But there were things she did not understand. Why did people who were not her boss keep telling her how they expected her to do her job? Why did people keep going to Steve for advice? He wasn't even a manager. And why did her immediate supervisor, Kelly Lorre, talk with her about how to dress for the office. She didn't think her skirt was too short or that she showed too much cleavage. That didn't have anything to do with her job anyway.

Marcus had been in the same job, the same position, for 12 years. He did a fine job, better than most people, even if he did say so himself, and he often did. Sure he had a few small performance bonuses but the big promotions, those that could move him to higher levels in the company, always evaded him. The last promotion went to Amber Conti, a truckler if there ever were one. Every time you turned around, she was sucking up to the bosses. It made Marcus wonder what you have to do to get ahead.

Laura has a new job but is clueless as to what is happening in the workplace around her. She does not understand how work groups influence their members, the importance of the impression she makes, and the nature of the informal organization. Marcus has been in the workforce for years, but apparently he still does not have any idea why things happen the way they do in the workplace. Opportunities pass him by. He has no sense of the positive value of networking, why networking is important, how perception affects so many outcomes, good and bad—and he might have a blind spot, something others see but he doesn't. Laura and Marcus actually have much in common. Laura and Marcus do not know how to decode the workplace. They do not understand the behavior of people around them or how others see them.

This book is about decoding the workplace, understanding the behavior of people in organizations. We spend most of our lives at work. Some people spend their work lives in the steel and glass of large corporations, others in the mills and factories of our towns and cities. We serve others for profit and not for profit. We heal the sick, make products, perform services, teach students, write reports, solve problems, make sales, wait tables, and flip burgers. For most of us, we awake in our homes, prepare for the day, then drive, ride, walk, or fly to a second "home"—functional or dysfunctional—where our hours are engaged.

What prepares us for this world of work? Education, vocational programs, training—both on and off the job—and apprenticeships. These are foundations, building blocks of knowledge, skills, and abilities to produce and perform in this world. Through our work experiences we build on these foundations. But are they sufficient to be successful or excel on the job? Perhaps for some, but for most I think not.

The world of work and the world of organizations are worlds of people. To succeed, to excel, or to simply have less stress in one's life, an understanding of people, as individuals and in groups, can be helpful. During the past century, sociologists, psychologists, and management scholars have studied the world of work. From Frederick Taylor's classic studies in the pig iron yards of Bethlehem Steel at the turn of the twentieth century to Elton Mayo's studies in the factory rooms of Western Electric's Hawthorne plant in the 1920s and 1930s; from Henry Mintzberg's research on CEOs to Fred Luthans's research in the offices of middle management; from Frank Gilbreth's studies of the laying of brick to Trist and Bamforth's work on the mining of coal; we have studied and learned about people at work. From studies in workplaces and in academic laboratories, our understanding of the behavior of people in organizations has grown. Textbooks on organizational behavior detail and summarize findings from thousands of studies conducted over the past 100 years.[1]

So much has changed during the past 100 years. Two World Wars were fought. A Cold War came and went. Nations have risen and fallen. Technology has advanced at a pace previously unimaginable. Men have walked on the moon. Your smart phone makes the tricorder from the 1960s futuristic TV show "Star Trek" almost seem obsolete. Television, the Internet, and globalization have changed our world. Although workplace activities and industries change, the fundamentals of human behavior do not. People are still people—with needs and wants and desires. We have more in common with our distant ancestors than we care to admit. When faced with perceived danger—be it real or imagined, such as an attacking tiger or a disliked boss—chemicals are released into our bloodstream. Our bodies prepare to fight or flee. Likewise, the underlying dynamics of human behavior hold true whether you work in a corporate office or at the local McDonald's.

This book is about fundamental things. Some of what follows might seem to be second nature or even common sense. But one person's "common sense" is not necessarily like another's. Somewhere in this book could be the one insight, the one idea, the one key that unlocks opportunity, the key that provides a solution, a plan, or a roadmap. That is my intent. To give you keys—to help you up your game, to enable you to decode the workplace and be more successful.

Throughout this book you will find keys. I use "keys" as a metaphor. Keys unlock things; the right key can help decode a program; a person with a key can unlock and see what others perhaps cannot. Keys can help to decipher the world around you, and suggest explanations, interpretations, or solutions.

The concepts and ideas you will find in these pages are indeed keys. I have clearly identified keys that I emphasize, but I expect you will find other keys that I have not highlighted, ideas or concepts highly relevant to your work life. The keys highlighted are those that I have found especially useful in decoding the workplace. They are grounded in theory and research and have practical applications for understanding workplace dynamics. Some of these keys will be new insights; others could be insights you intuitively understand but have implications which you have not considered. Regardless, how you use the key is what makes the difference—and that choice is yours.

Think of the keys as general guidelines. These guidelines hold true in most situations but not necessarily all. Can you perfectly understand the behavior of others around you? Of course not. Can you be better at it? Most likely. Most knowledge is probabilistic; that is to say, there are always exceptions. While in graduate school at Purdue, I made a bet with a professor. We were doing some research in which students had to rate images on whether they liked the image or disliked it. I thought I could find an image or images that everyone would like. Who would not like a gorgeous sunset? A smiling baby? A cute puppy? Well, it turns out that about 6% of the students in the study disliked these images. Using more than 200 images, 94% agreement was as good a result as I could get. Bet lost.

My suggestion is that as you read this book, reflect on how the keys and other concepts relate to your experiences. Do they help explain a situation or others' behaviors? Do they give you new insights, new ideas about your workplace, about yourself? Do they seem valid in your situation? I do not guarantee that all of the keys will fit your situation exactly. But the keys should help you to develop more accurate hypotheses about your workplace. Your hypotheses could be right or wrong, but by continuing to observe and reflect on the organizational life around you, there should be new insights. And you can adjust your hypotheses. These new insights then can inform your behavior, help with decisions you must make, and in most cases improve your effectiveness. Management scholars and corporate trainers agree that reflecting on one's workplace experiences can help a person perform more effectively.

> Gerald read this key: "It is important to be aware, as best you can, of the impressions that you create." Gerald had never given much thought to how he came across to others. He just did his job as well as he could, or at least he thought so. People in his office often had to give PowerPoint presentations about various projects to managers at higher levels. Although Gerald had much experience, he realized that he probably gave fewer presentations than anyone else in the office. He even helped others prepare their presentations but he didn't do the presenting. "Why?" he wondered. He really had not thought about it before. So Gerald talked with his boss.

> "I seem to get fewer opportunities to present to senior management. I was wondering if there was a reason why?"
> "Gerald, you are one of the best analysts on my team but you have an 'uh' problem."
> "An 'uh' problem?"
> "Yeah, I should have mentioned it to you sooner. I just never got around to it. You keep saying 'uh' all the time throughout your talks. It can be annoying."
> "Thanks for telling me. I had no idea. I'll see what I can do to fix that problem."

If Gerald had not thought about the impressions he created, he might never have talked with his boss or someone else, and his boss might never have told him about the issue, and instead just continued to assign him to "less-visible" presentations. Gerald had a friend video record one of his presentations. Gerald was stunned by what he saw. In every free space he inserted an "uh."

The fix was easy. Gerald practiced with a friend. Every time Gerald said "uh," his friend loudly said "No!" and then said, "Start over." It only took a few minutes for Gerald to become aware of what he was doing, and to become comfortable with the silence needed between sentences and thoughts. His boss noticed the difference and assigned Gerald higher-level presentations, which led to more opportunities.

Within these chapters you will find useful ideas. It is up to you to determine which of these will be of value to you.

CHAPTER TWO

Systems: Everything Is Connected

Jane enjoyed her position as a manager at TXZ Enterprises. When her company implemented a major change with new technology and new software, the employees Jane supervised no longer needed to talk with her as much. Her employees now had at their fingertips all the information they needed to make most decisions. Furthermore, using the new software Jane could more closely monitor the work of those she supervised.

The advantage to TXZ seemed obvious: "We don't need as many managers." TXZ downsized, eliminating half of the middle managers, and saved a lot of money. For the managers remaining, the number of people each supervised doubled. Jane was fortunate. She kept her job. But now, instead of managing 9 workers, she supervised 18 people.

At first, things at TXZ seemed to be going OK. A few office workers complained about more work and how they were now expected to do their jobs but most seemed satisfied with the change. It was several months before the first signs of problems appeared. Absenteeism and sick days started to increase—among the managers. Then turnover began. Managers were stressed and having difficulty adjusting to the job changes. Not only had the number of people reporting to them doubled, but also the managers' jobs became more difficult. Office workers handled most routine situations, but they took the toughest, thorniest problems they could not solve to their managers. Soon managers were overwhelmed with greater and more difficult workloads. Stress increased greatly.

Jane was no exception. At first it had not been difficult managing 18 employees. But as the months passed and her direct-report workers only came to her with the problems they could not solve, her work became more difficult, time-consuming, and stressful. All aspects of her life were affected. At a meeting of office managers, Jane's boss asked her to explain the decline in her unit's performance. Something snapped. Jane's heart raced wildly. She had difficulty breathing. She was rushed by ambulance to a local hospital.

Jane's situation, and that of the other managers at TXZ, could have been anticipated. The company had made the decision to downsize based only on financial analyses. It did not consider how the changes could negatively affect service and the human capital. Although financial analyses are critical, in many cases they are not sufficient. TXZ decision makers did not think through all of the potential implications of their actions. They did not consider the impact of the downsizing and the new technology on the various parts of the system. It was pretty much a bottom-line decision; it looked good on paper.

Organizations are systems. Activities, parts, and resources are interrelated and often are interdependent. Everyday people in workplaces are impacted by decisions in which they have no input or their input is ignored. Decisions that seem sound to the decision makers sometimes do not work out as expected. The problem typically is that decision makers are not taking a systems perspective. They are not thinking about, talking with, or listening to the other parts of the system which are affected by the decisions. The decision makers might not have any idea of how a decision made for one area impacts another area.

Key: Think of your workplace and the people in it as parts of systems, connected in ways that you can see and ways that you don't see.

Organizations are systems of interrelated and often interdependent parts. To decode the workplace, to have insights into what is happening around you, start with this key. The workplace is a system made up of smaller systems and is part of larger systems. This is a fundamental aspect of organizational life. Parts, activities, people, and resources are interrelated. Thinking about how aspects of the workplace are related to other aspects can give you insights. Who knows whom? How does my work affect other people? How is my work affected by activities in other parts of the organization? How is our organization affected by changes in the external environment, such as the economy, government, or changes in society?

Systems thinking can be powerful. Ludwig von Bertalanffy, a biologist, developed the tenets of General Systems Theory in the 1950s.[1] He noticed that his research was continually being affected by the research of other biologists. He realized that there was interdependence among biological research. Laws of growth and adaptation applied to all aspects of biology. Then it occurred to him that the same was true for all of existence.

Everything is part of a system. For Bertalanffy, a system was "any entity maintained by the mutual interaction of its parts, from atom to cosmos" and everything in between.[2]

We live our lives in systems but we rarely think about the systems. You are a biological organism with a circulatory system, respiratory system, nervous system, reproductive system, and others. Develop a problem breathing and you will think about your respiratory system. Develop a problem with your heart and you will think about your circulatory system. A system running smoothly probably will go unnoticed. A system that has a problem comes to the forefront. The same is true in the workplace.

You are a physical system composed of atoms and molecules. Atoms are more than 99.999% empty space; therefore you are composed mostly of nothing. You are a symbiotic system. Do you know what percent of the total cells in your body are actually human? About 10%.[3] Most of the cells in your body and on your body are microbes, such as bacteria and viruses, many of which depend on us for their existence. We need most of them. Likewise, the workplace is a system that depends on other systems, some obvious but others that might not be readily apparent.

You currently are sitting, standing, or lying somewhere on planet Earth and rotating—completing a full rotation every 24 hours. If you are at the equator, you are on a spinning top turning slightly more than 1,000 miles per hour. Unless you are standing at the North or South Pole, you are riding a top that is spinning at a tremendous speed. This spinning planet is moving around the sun at 67,000 miles per hour. The sun with its solar system in turn is moving through the Milky Way galaxy at 52,000 miles per hour. The Milky Way galaxy is moving at a whopping 1.3 million miles per hour toward what is being called "The Great Attractor," an area of the Universe that seems to be denser, and hence has greater gravity. And all of this is happening now—this very second. Take a deep breath.

We are bound to our planet by gravity. We only notice small changes. The Earth spins us around creating the appearance of celestial objects rising and setting as we rotate. We might see the sun's position in the sky change with the seasons. Or we could live our lives in such a way that we do not notice celestial changes. If you so choose, however, you can watch the moon rise or sun set and experience the grandeur of this solar system. Likewise, if you so choose, you can see aspects of your workplace that otherwise would go unnoticed.

Organizations are social systems. By attending to what goes on around us in the workplace, we can gain insights that we might otherwise miss, insights that might improve our job performance.

Bianca had been in her current position for more than a year. She worked mostly on her own. Occasionally she developed a productivity improvement proposal that she floated up her management chain. These would come back with a few comments but none were implemented.

One day Marissa invited Bianca to join her for lunch. Bianca always ate at her desk but decided today it might be good to go out. So Marissa and Bianca dropped by a local lunch spot popular with company employees. Bianca had never been there. While they were eating lunch, Bianca noticed that one of her coworkers, Juan, was sitting with the Assistant Vice President for Operations.

"That's Juan over there with the Ops guy, isn't it?" Bianca asked.
"Yeah, I often see them eating here. I heard their kids are on the same soccer team," replied Marissa.

The next time that Bianca had a productivity-improvement proposal, she discussed it with Juan. Juan liked the idea and agreed to support her. This time her proposal was accepted and implemented.

It is through interactions within a system that new system characteristics emerge. A system is more than the sum of its parts. It grows, adapts, or dies. Organizations that interact with their external environment and learn from changes in that environment are open systems.[4] They grow and adapt and are healthy. Organizations that do not interact and learn from environmental changes are not healthy and can die. In the early 1990s, there were successful CD music businesses with multiple operating locations. These chains of stores were great places to buy and listen to music. Today they are out of business. Most people buy music online. The environment changed.

How is your company functioning as a system? What about your workplace? Are you staying abreast of changes in your business and the external environment? Are you in a workplace that is proactive or one that just responds? The clues are all around you.

> **Key: If you have a systems perspective, then you probably will make better decisions.**

Thinking of organizations as being systems and integrating this perspective into your decision making can be a strength. Too often people see their parts of the organization as fiefdoms or silos separated from the rest of the organization. They do not consider how others are impacted by their decisions. Sometimes people do not take a systems perspective because they are concerned that it will take more time or more energy. I am not suggesting that all decisions you make should be from a systems perspective, but I am suggesting that you should use a systems perspective for the big decisions, the important decisions. Ask yourself and those in your group: Who is going to be affected by this decision? Do they need to be at the table? Do you need to get their inputs? Would their inputs improve the quality of the decision, the product, or the service? There are occasions when organizations could save much time and energy if they made those affected a part of the decision-making process.

> The prototype of the aircraft was sleek, fast, and fuel efficient. Potential sales were large. Nick was a late addition to the team evaluating the new aircraft. His job was to determine how much time and how many people would be needed to maintain the aircraft and then determine how much that maintenance would cost. To do so, Nick contracted with a company to simulate maintenance on the aircraft with efficiency experts timing the various tasks as they were being performed. Nick had difficulty comprehending the results. At least 25% of the routine maintenance activities required more time—and thus more manpower—than similar aircraft.
>
> To better understand why this was so, Nick and a small group of engineers who had designed some of the areas of the aircraft examined the prototype and the time-intensive maintenance activities. One maintenance task involved removing a component from the aircraft to make sure it was operating correctly. Removing this one component took more than 15 minutes and it took another 15 minutes to reinstall it. Nick asked the engineers to try removing this component.
>
> As the engineers worked on removing the component, they began to understand the problem—the task was difficult. Finally one of the engineers stated, "You know, if we would have thought about the folks who have to do this, we could have designed this differently. It really should not take more than five minutes to remove this component." The prototype showed that an otherwise great aircraft was going to be more costly to maintain simply because the engineers had not thought about the maintenance activities and how to make them easier to accomplish.

The engineers in this story were experts at designing aircraft systems but they omitted a critical element: the people who had to maintain the aircraft. They did not have a total systems perspective. My guess is that you have encountered this scenario as a consumer. I know I have. Products appear on the market that could be more consumer-friendly, such as electronic devices that have remote controls which seem to take forever to master. There have been many Christmas Eves when Santa had trouble following the directions to prepare a toy for the following morning's early risers. Any product or service can be improved when the consumer's input is included in product or service development.

I have been surprised in my consulting and managerial experience at how often managers make decisions without considering those who will be affected. The odds are significant that you will be impacted in the workplace by a decision for which the consequences were not foreseen. Imagine cylinders on a table where all the cylinders are connected with elastic bands. If you pull on one cylinder, the cylinders nearby are affected. But, actually, all of the cylinders are affected. The ones nearby are impacted the most, but the cylinders farthest away are pulled to some degree.

In making decisions we easily see the parts of the system affected most directly. It is more difficult to think about the more remote aspects of the system and how they might be affected. Get the right people around the table and you can make a better decision.

A systems perspective also can involve being aware of other systems. Sometimes we are unaware of systems that might be useful simply because we have not looked for them or asked the right people the right questions. During part of my Air Force career, I was responsible for maintaining certain data on Air Force personnel, including test scores on language proficiency. We maintained these scores in a master file of computerized personnel data. Want someone who can speak Spanish to do a particular job? Easy! I could have the names in minutes, if not seconds. So when an Air Force agency needed people who could speak Spanish, did it ask for a list? Nope. It did not realize that the system existed. Instead, planners went through names of personnel looking for people with an Hispanic surname who happened to do the type of work needed. Interesting approach but—as several people named "Garcia" might have told the agency—not everyone who has an Hispanic surname speaks Spanish or does so fluently.

> **Key: Never underestimate the importance of the informal systems or networks that exist in the workplace.**

The workplace has formal and informal systems. Sometimes these informal networks are called "informal organizations."[5] The formal system is prescriptive. It is how things work as stated by the organization in mission statements, plans, policies, procedures, and formal lines of authority. The informal organization is descriptive. It is how things actually work. This is a very powerful distinction. It is relatively easy to learn about the formal organization and how an organization says that it functions. Coming to understand the informal system and how things really work takes more time.

> Nara joined an office of 20 employees. All of their jobs were the same and were fairly routine. They processed a standard form submitted by many client businesses throughout the United States. Nara found the form to be cumbersome and fairly complex. Her job, like that of the other office employees, was to insure each form had been completed properly. She hoped to do well with this job and move on to bigger opportunities. After a week the office supervisor called her into his office.
>
> "Nara, we are glad to have you with us. Overall you are doing a good job. Just one area you need to work on. You are processing about 50% fewer forms per day than the other people in the office. You are going to need to increase that. Think you can do it?"
>
> Nara thought for a moment. She had no idea how she could do more than she was already doing, but she knew she had to try. "I am sure I can do better. Thank you for bringing this to my attention."
>
> Sally had been in the office for several years and seemed to process forms quickly. Nara approached her.
>
> "Sally, I was wondering if you could give me some pointers on checking these forms. It is taking me about 30 minutes for me to do one."
> "30 minutes? Oh, Nara. That just isn't good enough around here. Tell me what you do."
>
> Nara starting explaining in detail how she processed the form. Sally immediately saw the problem.
>
> "Nara, you are doing things by the book. No one here does that. If you do, you will get farther and farther behind. Some sections of the form you can pretty much ignore. They are not that important. We don't know why they don't change the form. In other parts you just need to look for a few key words. There are only three sections that you need to read carefully and think about. These."
>
> Nara thanked Sally and thought about what she had said. She was accustomed to doing things "by the book." But she needed to keep this job and Sally did seem to know what she was doing. So Nara took Sally's advice, processed the forms like the rest of the office did, and did so just as productively.

Nara's officemates had determined the most efficient way to process forms and get the job done to the satisfaction of the organization. They knew that some parts of the form were more critical than others and that some parts of the form—although completed—were rarely or never used. It is common for the informal organization to find ways to simplify work. Sometimes these ways of doing work eventually are incorporated into the formal procedures.

To decode the workplace, you need to understand the informal organization in your workplace. As a consultant, I studied the similarities and differences between the formal and informal systems in organizations. The Six-Box model developed by Marvin Weisbord is a useful guide for thinking about these similarities and differences.[6] At the heart of Weisbord's approach is comparing the formal system with the informal system on six dimensions—purposes, structure, rewards, relationships, helpful mechanisms, and leadership. For example, an organization might formally state that its purpose is to provide the best customer service in its business. Informally, however, the organization cuts corners in customer service to maximize its profits. Formally, senior leadership might create the appearance of a cohesive team when, in fact, informally the members of the senior leadership team are jockeying for power and influence with self-interest at the forefront. The gaps between the formal and the informal can be very revealing. Typically the smaller the gaps and the fewer the gaps, the more effective the organization. The more the values and purposes of the informal organization are aligned with the purposes and values of the formal organization, the stronger the organization. Much of the work of the organization is done through the informal organization through inter-relationships and interdependencies.

Being aware of the systems around you in the workplace—both formal and informal—can help you understand the behavior of others. Notice what happens around you. Think about relationships among people, among parts of the organization, and with the external environment. Use systems thinking in your decision making. Observe who has a systems perspective and who does not.

The concepts in this book can be found in both the formal and informal organizations. The keys help you decode both. You might have a designated manager with formal authority but the real leader of your workplace might not be in a position of authority. Some of your coworkers might have little influence in the day-to-day running of the workplace but have much influence informally in determining what really happens. As you encounter the keys and concepts, think about how they apply to the systems of which you are a part.

I never knew Neil Armstrong, the first person to set foot on the moon. But I admired him. I did see him once, at a graduation ceremony at Mount St. Joseph University where I am on the faculty. He was the graduation speaker. I kept looking at his feet trying to remember which one was the first on the Moon, left or right? Later I Googled the answer. It was his left.

Neil Armstrong was an engineer. In piloting aircraft and spacecraft, he studied and understood their systems. Three times his knowledge of systems saved his life.[7] In 1966, he was the command pilot on Gemini VIII with pilot David Scott. The spacecraft went into a violent, dangerous spin—almost one revolution per second—which could have caused the astronauts to black out. Armstrong diagnosed the situation, found a solution, and brought the spacecraft under control. In 1968, Armstrong was practicing for the moon landing using the Lunar Landing Training Vehicle here on Earth. The Lunar Landing Training Vehicle suddenly lost the pressure that controlled the steering jets. Armstrong knew immediately that he had to eject, and he did. His parachute opened only seconds before he touched the ground. In 1969, during the first descent to land on the moon, the Lunar Excursion Module (LEM) computers were taking Armstrong and fellow astronaut Buzz Aldrin into a field of boulders where an attempted landing would have ended in disaster. Armstrong took manual control and piloted the LEM to a different location. The LEM landed safely with only seconds of fuel remaining.

In this chapter we have discussed the workplace and organizations as social systems. This, too, Neil Armstrong understood. After the moon landing he lived a life of great humility, unwilling to cash in on his well-earned fame. He knew—he understood—that he and Buzz Aldrin were just the most visible members of the Apollo program to put people on the Moon, that tens of thousands of engineers and other workers—who would never receive fame—made Apollo 11 happen. Armstrong knew that he was part of something far bigger than himself—and he never failed to give credit to others. He knew that he was just one part of a system that made landing on the moon a reality.

Part II: Individual Differences

CHAPTER THREE

Perception: Don't Assume That Others See the Workplace as You Do

Aiden and Sophia had just finished watching a movie on Netflix.

"Now that was a great movie," said Sophia. "I sure am glad we chose that one."

"Great? Are you kidding? That was one of the worst movies I have seen in years. How could you possible think that was a great movie?"

"I liked the characters, the way they interacted, and the lead guy was easy on the eyes."

"But the editing was horrid, the dialogue trite. It was painful to watch. What a waste of time."

Aiden and Sophia viewed the exact same movie, but their perceptions of the movie were very different. Differing perceptions happen frequently in our daily lives. Nearly every sporting event has at least one moment when a call is disputed and the two sides see it differently. Attend any youth soccer game and listen to the parents on either side of the field. The same thing happens in the workplace. People see things differently. Sometimes we know that, but other times we do not have a clue.

Our world is a perceptual world. Your reality and my reality are not the same. We see the world through different lenses constructed by our experiences, learning, and inferences. Intuitively we know this. We see conflicts resulting from different views of the same reality all the time in our workplaces, our homes, our communities, our nations, and our world.

Key: People see the world differently.

"Duh," you say. "I know this. So what's new?" Sure, but does it affect how you see and understand what goes on around you? Cognitively we understand this but behaviorally and emotionally we forget. This is not rocket science, but it might as well be.

We insist that our view is the correct view: "I don't know why you can't see it; it's as plain as the nose on your face." We act as if everyone sees things the way we do: "I'm sure we all agree this is the way to do it." We fail to consider how others might perceive our actions: "How can he possibly be upset with what I did? What's there to be upset about?" We get upset when others do things differently than we would have done them: "Why on earth would she do that? That doesn't make any sense at all!"

To decode the workplace, we start by understanding the significance and power of perceptions—and that your perceptions are yours, and might not be the perceptions of others. Sometimes your perceptions will agree with those of other people; sometimes they won't. But we never should just assume that another person shares our view.

The implications of this cannot be overstated. How you view the world and how others view you in the world will determine much of your success at work and in life. Perceptions affect job opportunities, relationships, performance, promotions, physical health, mental health, and more. All of the concepts in this book are ultimately perceptual.

Consider the job search. How do you go about getting a job? Whether you apply online, by mail, or in person, you are telling others about yourself. A resume, for example, says more about you than what is stated in words on a page. It reveals your ability to communicate in writing, your attention to detail, and your ability to organize facts cogently and succinctly. It is an example of the quality of your work. In short, it leads to a perception of you. Even if it is being scanned electronically, someone eventually will read it. Likewise, what you do with that resume can form an impression. Do you email or mail it and cross your fingers, or do you research the company and then find a way to deliver it personally to someone in the organization?

What about the image you project in cyberspace? What impressions might be created by your profile image on Facebook? That cool selfie for your friends might prevent you from being hired for a job. Do you have a presence on LinkedIn, increasingly the place where professionals connect online and recruiters search? What impressions might a person get from viewing your LinkedIn page? Do you have a photo? Does your profile contain misspelled words? Does it create the impression of someone a company might want to interview or do business with? Conversely, what impression do you create by not having a LinkedIn profile? Recently I was at a meeting with professionals from many different organizations. The topic turned to recruiting. When the speaker for the evening asked how many used LinkedIn for recruiting, more than 75% of the 100-plus people present raised their hands. When asked if they ever checked Facebook pages to see how applicants present themselves, nearly every hand went up.

When you do get an interview, the interviewers' perceptions of you and your fit with the organization will most likely determine your possibilities. How are you dressed? How do you stand, sit, talk, and conduct yourself? The interviewer is forming impressions. Similarly, you are forming impressions about this company and considering how you might fit, if given the chance. Prepare for interviewing with someone who will give you candid feedback. There often are simple things that are easy to overlook. Do you smoke? If so, then your clothes might smell of cigarettes. If so, you might not be hired for a job and not even know that was the reason. The smell identified you as a smoker. Some companies will see you as potentially contributing to greater health insurance costs. Others might think you would be less productive on the job because you will take smoking breaks.

Throughout your career people's perceptions of you—accurate or not—largely determine your opportunities. In our workplaces, people meet and interact. You will be sized up by others, fit into some useful stereotype, and be pegged there unless significant conflicting information comes to light.

> Harry was being considered for a vice president position at a major company. The CEO invited Harry to his home for dinner. The food was fabulous and the table formally set with silverware, fine china, and crystal glassware. Unfortunately, Harry used the wrong fork at the wrong time. He used his dessert fork for his salad. Harry flunked. The CEO remarked to a friend, "I'm not promoting anyone to VP who doesn't know his way around a dinner table."

Harry potentially could have been a tremendous asset as a VP in this company but he'll never know. The CEO perceived Harry as not having what it takes to succeed in the position because Harry used the wrong fork. As a vice president Harry would attend many formal dinners. The CEO was concerned that Harry might embarrass the company. Perceptions of behaviors this small and seemingly insignificant can make or break careers. The CEO's perception was that Harry didn't have the "right stuff." Sometimes critical perceptions go beyond your immediate workplace behaviors but might impact your workplace opportunities.

The young army major knew she had what it takes to become a high-ranking general officer someday. She knew the odds were slim but she had her act together. Her boss, a colonel, agreed. She asked the colonel, "What do you think my odds are of being promoted to general someday?"

The colonel replied, "Zero, unless you can get your husband to change his behaviors. As a general officer, you and your husband would be a team. Frankly, he drinks too much, talks too much, and offends people."

The major knew that her boss was right. Her husband had changed over the years; he was not the same man that she'd married. She had tried to get him to change, to get help with his drinking problem, but nothing happened. She weighed her choices, tried harder to help her husband, but finally gave up and divorced him. In a few years she was promoted to the high rank of general officer.

There's an assumption rooted in the American workplace that hard work and good work are rewarded. This is not necessarily the case. There are millions of hardworking Americans who do the yeoman work of the nation and are treated no differently than other "workers" who produce less and do not work as hard. Where objective measures of output or quality of work exist, the probability of just reward is higher. In the knowledge-related and white-collar positions of our workforce, this probability is reduced and problematic.

> **Key: Promotions and opportunities are not based on you and your performance but on perceptions of you and your performance.**

You might be the best person who has ever occupied the position you have at your company. You could run circles around your nearest competitor for advancement. But unless your superiors have the same perceptions, it probably will not make any difference.

Who does get ahead? In the 1980s, Fred Luthans of the University of Nebraska-Lincoln and his associates studied this question.[1] They found that managers spend their time performing four types of activities: communicating (that is, exchanging information, paperwork); traditional management activities (such as planning, controlling, making decisions); human resource management (motivating, disciplining, managing conflicts); and networking (interacting with others, socializing, politicking). At this point, you probably can guess what they found when they studied nearly 250 managers to see who got ahead. The managers who were most successful in moving to higher levels were the managers who spent more time networking than time doing the other three activities. What about effectiveness on the job? Based on the perceptions of subordinates and subordinates' reported levels of job satisfaction, the most effective managers spent most of their time communicating and working people issues. Fewer than 10% of the managers were both successful and highly effective.

Effective employees do not necessarily get promoted. People higher up must get to know you. Part of the job of a manager is keeping an eye out for talent. People who network and naturally have or have chosen to develop social skills have a higher probability of advancing, all things being equal.

We form perceptions about other people, and they form perceptions about us. Over repeated interactions, our perceptions and their perceptions either are validated or changed. When decision makers are looking at people for promotions and other opportunities, it is more likely they will go with someone about whom they have a positive impression— often impressions formed through interactions, the heart of the process of networking.

Does this mean how you do your job is not important? Of course it is important. Work can be full of intrinsic (the feeling of a job well done, meeting a challenge, contributing, making a difference) as well as extrinsic (making a living, supporting others, keeping a job) satisfactions. But doing your job well is not necessarily sufficient for advancement.

Key: Be aware, as best you can, of the impressions that you create.

How do others see you? How do you come across to your coworkers, your subordinates, your boss, and your customers? Some companies are using 360-degree feedback in which your peers, direct reports, supervisor, and sometimes customers are asked questions about your performance. This feedback is used for development, which can be good, and sometimes it is used in appraisals, which can be more problematic. Although this feedback system might have benefit (depending on how it is administered and used, and the level of trust and openness in the organization), it is different from what I am suggesting here. The 360-degree feedback system is a formal organizational approach to gathering information about performance. What I am suggesting is an informal personal approach, a mindset to become aware and maintain awareness of how you are perceived.

Every day, as we interact with others, there is much information about ourselves that we simply do not pay attention to or which we ignore.

Why? We have things on our mind. We are trying to get the job done. We are too busy to think about our behaviors and others' reactions to them. In so doing, we ignore valuable information that could make us more effective. Management scholars from Mary Follett in the 1920s to Douglas McGregor in the 1960s to Henry Mintzberg today, have advocated that we be self-reflective and analyze our experiences. In 1925 Follett stated, "To know what principles may underlie any given activity of ours is to take a conscious attitude toward our experience."[2]

So what information are we ignoring? Consider the following questions. What happens when you suggest an idea at a meeting? Is it well received, debated, considered, or is it quickly dismissed or put aside—or worse, is it picked up by someone else who champions it and gets the credit? What is the body and facial language of others when you are engaged in conversation? Do people listen to you or are they looking for an excuse to end the conversation? Are there differences in how men and women respond to your workplace behaviors? Do people find you pleasant, abrasive, receptive, or arrogant? Do people like to work with you? Do they seek you out to ask your opinion? Do you have credibility? Are you trustworthy? Are you the last to know what is really happening in your workplace? What do you really know about how other people see you?

"Why should I care?" you might say. "I am who I am. Take it or leave it." If you have no desire to be a more effective or successful employee or manager in working with others, so be it. But most of us work in organizations—large and small—with other people. Work gets done by people working together. If you have a better idea of how others see you, then you can make better decisions that make you more effective. You don't have to change who you are but you might want to change some of your behaviors.

> Ted was seen as aloof and not interested in the people he managed. He was technically proficient, his decisions usually were on the money, but his subordinates and coworkers did not enjoy working with him. His direct reports accomplished the requirements of their jobs, but they had no desire to go beyond that. Ted was all business. No one had ever seen Ted laugh or smile. He had never even asked anyone how things were going.
>
> When a consultant brought these insights to Ted's attention, he replied, "I've never really thought about that before. I guess I'm just so busy I don't let up."
>
> In the weeks that followed, Ted slowly started to interact on a more personal level with those around him and even smiled occasionally. Over time Ted's image changed. He was still the same hard worker but people viewed him as more accessible and friendlier. Now they were more willing to go the extra mile for him.

Ted had a blind spot, something that others saw in his behavior that he didn't see. In his case it was a negative blind spot. Some blind spots are positive, for example people who are always helpful, never complaining, seemingly at peace with themselves and the world, or who just make work a better place by their presence but don't have a clue that their positive spirits lift the spirits of those around them. The examples that readily come to mind, however, usually are negative blind spots. Most of us have known people who just make us scratch our heads. People who always come across as if they know everything but don't; people who obviously and continually "suck up" to their bosses; people nobody wants to work with because they are quick tempered, unpleasant, or just plain difficult. We've seen them. We know them. We might be one of them. We all have blind spots.

The idea of blind spots is part of an organizational development heuristic called the "Johari Window" (pronounced "joe-harry" after Joe Luft and Harry Ingram who developed it in the 1950s).[3] We all have aspects of ourselves that we reveal to others. My students know about aspects of my life because I weave examples from my life into lecture and discussion to illustrate course concepts. But there are parts of my life that remain "hidden" or private—that I choose not to share. Likewise, there are aspects of my behavior that are blind spots, things about me that other people see but about which I am not aware.

For years I wore a brown corduroy jacket with patches on the elbows everywhere I went. I loved it. It was me. Then at a party one evening an acquaintance pointed out that I needed to upgrade my wardrobe, that I risked the possibility of not being taken seriously by some people of means with whom I potentially would be conducting business. I did not like the idea of being judged by what I wore. My attitude was, to quote Henry David Thoreau, "If I am not I, who will be."[4] But I recognized the wisdom of that counsel, I upgraded my look, and I must admit that I noticed a difference in how people responded to me.

Shortly thereafter, at a conference in New York City, I approached the speaker for the afternoon, a government official of high rank, an advisor to presidents. He had delivered a provocative address and I had a question. He was in a group surrounded by other professors. I walked up to ease into the group and take my turn but he stopped the conversation with the others, turned to me, introduced himself, and shook my hand. We chatted, he answered my questions, and then he turned back to the others. As I pondered this, I realized that the other professors were dressed as I had been dressed only a month before. In my Brooks Brothers suit I now was in a corporate uniform for America, dressed similarly to the speaker and not like the others. It was a powerful lesson.

Sometimes being aware of another person's blind spots can be helpful. The boss who always has a twitch below his right eye when he is being less than honest—but doesn't know he has this twitch. That "tell" provides useful insights, both in the workplace or when playing poker with him.

How do you find out if you have any blind spots? This can be difficult. You have to be willing to listen openly and without criticism to someone you trust who knows and values you.

Charlotte knew that she was less effective in her workplace than she could be. If anyone talked with her, it was because she initiated the conversation, except for Ava. Charlotte and Ava had known each other for several years. They had graduated from the same college a few years apart, but that was enough for them to form a bond.

After a company training presentation on the Johari Window, Charlotte decided to ask Ava about her blind spots. She trusted Ava. Charlotte found the opportunity one day after work when no one else was around.

"Ava, I need to talk with you about something and just keep it between the two of us."

"Sure." ·

"I was just wondering. How do I come across around here? I trust your opinion and I really want to know. I don't want to know who says what and all that. I just want to know how I'm perceived here in the workplace."

"Are you sure you want to talk about this?"

"Yes, I do."

"Well, OK. If you're sure. Truthfully, you come across a little too self-centered. I know you and I know you're not, but when you talk it's usually about yourself and what you've done and what you like. And once you start talking you usually don't give anyone a chance to join in. Look, I like you, but that's the way it is."

"Thanks, Ava. You're a pal."

Charlotte pondered Ava's remarks. She trusted Ava and valued her judgment. "Self-centered; talk too much," she thought. "I can work on this." And she did. When Charlotte caught herself going on and on about herself, she would stop, pause, and listen to the other person. She worked hard at changing this behavior and the perceptions of her, and in time she was successful.

Negative blind spots can end careers and deny opportunities. What are yours?

For years I had negative feelings about the term "impression management," but I came to realize that awareness of the impressions you create is important. Like it or not, as Shakespeare wrote in, "As You Like It," "All the world's a stage, and all the men and women merely players." Erving Goffman, the sociologist, expounded on this idea in *The Presentation of Self in Everyday Life*, a treatise on how we communicate, verbally and nonverbally, as we move through our life's play.[5] He argued that regardless of whether we are aware of it, we all are actors in a performance, choosing what we share, when we share, how we share, forming impressions. A visit to a singles bar on a Saturday night is ample proof.

To decode the workplace, we must understand that we live in a world of perceptions. To be more effective, we need to be aware of the impressions we create. Some of us are naturally self-monitoring, learning about ourselves from the reactions of those around us. Some of us are not, but we can learn to self-monitor. We can develop hypotheses about the effects of our actions and make adjustments—and through trial and error elevate our interpersonal skills and effectiveness in the workplace.

CHAPTER FOUR

Motivation: It's Not All about Money

For two decades Dave had been at the same job. He worked with six guys loading containers of grocery items into trailers for large trucks to deliver to grocery stores regionally. The work was steady. The pay was reasonable. Then Dave hit the state lottery jackpot, a cool $10 million dollars after taxes. Dave quit his job.

A month later Dave showed up at the loading docks. "Hi, guys, I'm back," he said with a big grin. His coworkers were stunned.

"What do you mean you're back? Dude, you're a millionaire."

"Yeah, Dave, what the heck are you doing here?"

Dave still smiling just looked at his old buddies and said, "I missed you guys."

If you won millions of dollars in a lottery, would you continue to work? Think about it. I often pose this question to my students. Some say, "Are you crazy? Of course, not." Others, "Maybe but I'd do some traveling first." Still others, "Yes, but I'd work elsewhere, start my own business, or do volunteer work." And still others, "Probably, I'm not sure what else I would do with my time." Do people who win large sums of money in lotteries continue to work? Research studies have answered this. The majority do continue to work. Some studies suggest that more than 85% do so.[1]

People work for several reasons. The most fundamental reason is economic. In most societies, people need income to buy goods and services. We need a paycheck and want benefits that allow us to enjoy life. In a tough economy there are many people who just want a job—any job—that can put a roof over their heads and food on the table. Clearly that is not the case for big lottery winners, at least not for those who manage their winnings. Dave went back to work because he missed his buddies. We are social animals. We need other people. The workplace can be like a second family, be it functional or dysfunctional. We have social needs that often are met in the workplace. We interact with others, form friendships, and make acquaintances. For many people, we find part of our identity in what we do in our jobs. We see how the work we do benefits others, is part of a larger and meaningful enterprise, and gives us a sense of accomplishment. For some people, work also can provide a sense of place in community or a perception of status, especially for those in professional positions such as teachers, doctors, lawyers, and religious leaders.

> **Key: Work is more than a paycheck; we have various needs that can be satisfied in the workplace.**

People have needs, physiological and psychological, that affect behaviors, consciously and unconsciously. Most needs can be thought of as deficient conditions that we seek to satisfy. When I am hungry, I need food, I find something to eat. Needs do not differentiate between whether you are at home, the workplace, or elsewhere. When you are hungry, you are hungry. As human beings, our needs are just part of us. We vary in which needs are most important at any given time or part of our life but, regardless, our work and the workplace can figure importantly in need satisfaction.

Douglas McGregor wrote about human needs and their role in the workplace in *The Human Side of Enterprise*.[2] In this book, McGregor discussed lower-level needs (physiological, safety) and higher-level needs (social, esteem, and self-fulfillment), and how the workplace should provide opportunities to help people meet lower- and higher-level needs. If this sounds familiar, it probably is. At the end of the chapter, McGregor listed his references, acknowledging the classic work of Abraham Maslow.[3]

Using Maslow's hierarchy of needs in decoding the workplace is different from how one might think it would be used. From a workplace perspective, Maslow's theory is not really about the individual. If you are second-guessing where someone is on Maslow's hierarchy, then you are missing the point. The workplace implication is that organizations should recognize that people have different needs and companies should provide a variety of programs that can benefit employees no matter where they are in Maslow's hierarchy.

Therefore, if I ran an organization, I might greet a meeting of new employees as follows.

Welcome to Ballard Enterprises! We are so glad you have joined our team. Here at Ballard, you'll find that we put you first; we understand you have a variety of needs, and we work hard to help you meet those needs. We have an excellent cafeteria with great selections every day. And you don't have to walk a mile to find a clean, convenient restroom. At Ballard, our selection process does take several months, but now that you are hired—and once you pass the six-month review—we guarantee a job for as long as you want it. If that means offering to retrain you at some point, we'll do it. We reimburse educational tuition at 100%. Our safety record is second to none. We have the lowest accident record in the state in our industry and great health benefits. And we have fun. Want to line dance? Want to bowl? Our co-ed softball team won the city championship last year. Want to be recognized for your achievements? We have fair and competitive opportunities for advancement and pay raises. We have programs for Employee of the Month, Employee of the Quarter, Employee of the Year, Five-Year Employee Achievement, and others. You are not a number. You are a person, a valued employee. You can be all that you can be at Ballard Enterprises.

Is this approach practical? Perhaps for some organizations, but probably not for most. But the perspective that employees can be motivated by different things is very important. Maslow saw the human potential in each of us. He often questioned his graduate students, asking each something to the effect, "What great book are you going to write? What great accomplishment are you going to achieve?"

People's needs, wants, and desires figure prominently in theories of motivation. "Motivation is that which energizes, directs, and sustains behavior," so stated Richard Steers.[4] This is my favorite definition of motivation. It energizes. (What do you need, want, desire? What gets you going?) It directs. (Toward what? To what end?) It sustains. (What keeps you going? How do you persevere?) These are the components of motivation. What truly motivates you? What will you put energy into making happen?

The people around you in the workplace are there for a variety of reasons. Money and social needs, sure, but beyond that, what motivates them? Frederick Herzberg proposed that there are factors that reduce job dissatisfaction but do not motivate, such as job security, pay, and benefits, and there are motivating factors that affect our job satisfaction, such as feelings of accomplishment and recognition.[5] Research has not supported the details of Herzberg's theory.[6] Even so, Herzberg did make an important contribution. His research showed that how we perceive our jobs—the nature of the work itself—affects our motivation. Do we have a sense of accomplishment, are we recognized for our efforts, do we enjoy the work at hand?

Jasmine did not like her job. She worked as a desk clerk at a large hotel. She wanted to work in the hospitality industry and this was the only position she was offered. The job had potential. She also met interesting people (well, mostly). Sometimes Jasmine could do small things to make a difference for the people who stayed at the hotel. Her frustrations were when the problems were not small: a room that was not cleaned; a reservation that was messed up; a customer who was very unhappy for a very good reason. Unfortunately, Jasmine could do little to address such issues. She did not have the authority to make adjustments to room rates, provide dining coupons, or even award extra bonus points to longtime customers. Her supervisor had to approve all such actions, and sometimes her supervisor was difficult to reach.

When the hotel—part of a larger chain—got a new VP of Operations, things changed. After a review of existing policies, management of the hotel chain gave experienced frontline employees authority to make the decisions formerly reserved for supervisors. Jasmine was empowered. She now could evaluate situations and provide better customer service. She could treat people the way she would like to be treated. She liked her job.

Empowering employees by enriching jobs and giving more responsibility can be motivating. But it's important to understand that not all people want their jobs enriched. Think about your job. Is it motivational? Do you enjoy the job itself? Do you get a sense of accomplishment from your work? What about those around you in the workplace? Are they motivated by what they do? What would you change, if anything, about your work? What about your workplace?

> **Key: Your perception as to whether you are being treated fairly can have a significant effect on your motivation.**

The sense of fair treatment is a huge factor. In my opinion, one of the two most applicable theories of motivation is J. Stacy Adams's equity theory.[7] People want to be treated fairly. Although organizations should try to treat each employee fairly, the key is the employee's perception. A person could be being treated fairly, and be seen by coworkers as being treated fairly, but if a person does not think he or she is being treated fairly, then that person's motivation most likely will be low. The reverse is also true. Unfair treatment will not affect motivation if it is not seen as unfair treatment. One obvious implication is that there will be times that, no matter how fairly a manager treats someone, the employee might not see the manager as being fair. In the workplace you often can determine who perceives their situation as unfair from their words and actions.

According to equity theory, motivation is about your perceptions of what you bring to the workplace (inputs) and what you get out of the workplace (outcomes) and how these inputs and outcomes in your estimation compare with those of others. Inputs vary from person to person. Do you think you bring a good, relevant education to the workplace? Useful experiences, skills, or knowledge? A team spirit? A "can do" attitude? A strong work ethic? The ability to learn quickly? What are the qualities that you think you bring to the workplace which make you a valuable employee? Likewise, the outcomes we desire will vary. Some outcomes will be extrinsic, such as fair pay, job security, an opportunity for advancement, or a pleasant work environment. Others will be intrinsic, such as job satisfaction, recognition for a job well done, a feeling of accomplishment, or personally meaningful work.

Regardless of whether we are aware of it, we compare ourselves with other people. A person with whom we compare ourselves is what Adams called a "referent." As the social psychologist Leon Festinger described many years ago, we are social animals who by our very nature are continually comparing ourselves with others.[8] We observe others and compare this information with ourselves. In the workplace your referent could be a coworker or coworkers, a friend, family member, or even yourself as you recall your work and rewards in a previous job. We go through life comparing our inputs and outcomes with our referent's inputs and outcomes. If they do not match up well, then it can affect motivation.

> Chris thought that he brought a lot of experience to his job in marketing, at least as compared with Evan, who had the same job. Chris worked hard, worked smart, and got results. He enjoyed the work. Even though his supervisor thought he was a good worker, Chris did not get the recognition he thought he deserved, especially as compared with Evan. Evan appeared to contribute less to the business but seemed to get more rewards—the best business trips, pay increases, and even a promotion. Seeing Evan promoted was too much for Chris to handle. Fed up with the unfairness of it all, he resigned and took a marketing position elsewhere.

For most of us, when we compare our inputs and outcomes with others, if the scale is not even, we are less motivated. Chris saw himself having high input with low outcomes whereas he perceived Evan has having low input and high outcomes. Chris's perceived input/outcome ratio does not match up well with Chris's perception of Evan's input/outcome ratio. This perceived difference creates psychological tension that, over time, we try to resolve. Chris resolved this tension by leaving the company, but there are other ways to do so. One method is to play mental games with ourselves, change how we view things. "I guess I really did not do as good a job as I thought I was doing." "That promotion just wasn't that big a deal." Or we might change our input, such as getting more education or working harder. Or we even might change the outcome.

> Mario was hired into a company along with two other employees who had similar positions. After a year, the other two new hires received pay increases and the company then hired three more people. Two years after Mario was hired, all five of the other employees got a pay raise. Mario figured he just had to work harder. Three years after Mario had been hired, the other five employees received yet another pay increase. Mario had had enough. He scheduled a meeting with his supervisor.
> "I've been here three years. The people hired when I was hired have received three pay increases. Even the people hired after me have received pay increases. My work is just as good as any of them and I have never received a pay increase," Mario stated.
> "You have never asked for one," his supervisor replied.

I have wondered what took Mario so long, but such things do happen. Mario got a catch-up pay raise. There is another way to resolve the tension from inequity that I think has wide application for our lives. Change your referent. You can use comparisons with referents to elevate your performance or strengthen your resolve. But you also can make your life miserable by comparing yourself or your life with the wrong referent or referents.

I received my doctorate at Purdue University. My fellow graduates have gone on to distinguished careers at research universities, as endowed chairs, in leadership positions of major professional organizations, and have successfully climbed the corporate ladder to financial riches. Had these been my pursuits and had I fallen short, having chosen these referents I would have regrets and be less satisfied with my life. But they are not my referents. I love what I do and my academic home. I know there are many people with doctorates who would like to have full-time academic positions but do not. So I am thankful.

I have known several people who have gone through their lives making themselves miserable because they were trying to measure up to a high bar set by a parent, a relative, a friend—and in their estimation they were always falling short. Think about your referents. Some will change over time. Others might not. Who are you comparing yourself to in the workplace? How does that affect your behaviors? What about in life? Identifying your referents and evaluating your choice of those referents could be beneficial.

> **Key: When you believe that your effort will get the job done satisfactorily and lead to outcomes you desire, you are more likely to be motivated.**

This might seem like a straightforward statement but it actually is packed with implications for understanding your motivation and that of others. It is especially useful in evaluating the effectiveness of managers. This is the basis of the other theory of motivation that I have found to be very practical—Victor Vroom's expectancy theory.[9] Here's a very simplified version in a nutshell.

$$M = E \times I \times V$$

Here, M is motivation, E is expectancy, I is instrumentality, and V is valence. If either expectancy, instrumentality, or valence is low, then motivation will be low.

"Expectancy" is about how you see the relationship between your effort and your performance. It could be that you can do your job at an acceptable level of performance with no problems. Conversely, you might think that, no matter how hard you try, you will never be able to get the job done well enough to meet your organization's stated requirements or satisfy your boss.

> Latanya was frustrated. It took her forever to get a job in a call center and now she wasn't measuring up. Her boss told her that her quality ratings were good but she was taking too long with each customer. The call center expected each agent to answer ten calls per hour. Usually it took her ten minutes to resolve an issue for a customer. On her best day, Latanya handled only seven calls per hour. Latanya's boss offered her another week of training. She agreed but she seriously doubted that she would ever be able to average ten calls per hour.

Latanya's boss clearly identified the level of performance expected. When Latanya did not meet the standard, he got her additional training. He was trying to help her succeed. But Latanya did not think she could do it. Her expectancy was very low; thus her motivation was very low.

There are numerous reasons why you might have low expectancy. Maybe the level of performance is just too high. Perhaps you do not have the necessary training or skills. It might be work for which you do not have the aptitude.

In high school I was hired to work in a television repair shop. My boss tried to teach me basic electrical concepts to diagnose and repair TVs but I just didn't get it. I only lasted a few months at the job. While studying at the United States Air Force Academy, I was required to take a couple courses in electrical engineering, "double E." My expectancy was low, and so were my grades.

Good managers let you know what level of performance is required. They give you feedback and tell you whether you are meeting that level. If not, the better managers will try to help you attain that level of performance. Of course, if your manager does not clarify the level of performance needed or give you feedback, then you might need to figure things out for yourself, talk to other employees, or ask your manager.

"Instrumentality" is how you perceive the relationship between your level of performance and some outcome that you desire. Do you think that your level of performance will be instrumental in helping you attain the outcome you want?

> Ashley rose to the top of middle management at her company, an international enterprise. By all measures her career was a success. Her performance continued to be outstanding but she felt her opportunities were limited. Ashley wanted to demonstrate her leadership at a higher level, to move to senior management. She was ready. The time was now. But Ashley did not think this could happen. Her company had never had a woman as a senior manager. Those positions went to members of the "old boy" network. She was looking at the glass ceiling. So when the corporate headhunters came calling, she listened, she interviewed, and she moved to a VP position at another company.

Ashley had reached a point in her career at which her instrumentality was low, and hence her motivation was not what it had once been. Her chain of command either did not understand what Ashley wanted or they were not willing to make that outcome happen. In reality, most of us will have a variety of outcomes we desire from our jobs, not just one. Some outcomes will be extrinsic (e.g., pay, job security, promotions) and others will be intrinsic (e.g., feelings of a job well done, being appreciated).

There are two important implications for managers here. First, managers should make clear the link between performance and outcomes. Second, managers, whenever possible, should know their direct reports well enough to have some idea what they really want. The greater the number of direct reports (span of control), the more difficult this becomes.

My consulting experience and my graduate students from corporate America suggest that it is in this part of expectancy theory that managers need to improve. As one Fortune 500 VP told me after a presentation on expectancy theory, "We're pretty good on the first part of this theory but we fall on our face here. We really do not do a good job showing how performance leads to rewards, especially ones people want." My opinion is that managers who buy into these two points and execute them through their actions potentially will be more successful. A manager cannot always deliver on what an employee might want, such as a promotion or better office, but the act of trying can make a difference to the employee. The more powerful the supervisor, the more likely the desired outcome can be achieved.

These two points served me very well in my years as a manager. I talked with my direct reports. I listened. Then I made clear the level of performance I expected, and that if workers gave me that level of performance, I would do my best to help them achieve that which they desired. Sometimes I was successful, sometimes not—but it was clear to me that these efforts motivated those who worked for me. Knowing what an individual actually wants—not what you think the individual wants—is important.

"Valence" is how much an employee values or desires the outcome or outcomes associated with their level of performance. In some occupations, job security might be sufficient, highly valued, or a steady paycheck. In others—in especially those fields where it is easy to find jobs—perhaps less so. I have known people who took lateral positions—same pay, same type of work—simply because their new companies offered great tuition-reimbursement programs. Support in obtaining more education had a high valence. My experience as a manager is that you have to know your employees well enough to know their desired outcomes.

Tomas loved playing softball. Now middle-aged, he had played on softball teams for most of his life. He was very well respected as a player on church and community teams and was noticed by the Hawks, the top amateur team in the city. The Hawks asked him to join their team, a significant honor in local softball circles. There was only one problem: To get to the Hawks' practices on Thursdays, Tomas would need to leave an hour early from his job.

Tomas thought about the offer, how much he would love to play with the Hawks, and he found the courage to approach his boss.

"Sir, you know how much I like playing softball. I just got an offer to play with the Hawks. They are by far the best team in the city."
"Tomas, good for you. I know that will be a lot of fun."
"Sir, there is a problem though. They have to practice early on Thursdays. Has to do with the field being available."
"How early?"

"Well, to get there in time for practice, I'd need to leave here about an hour early."

Tomas's boss thought for a moment.

"Tomas, you are a fine employee. Tell you what. If you can make up that hour on another day and give me the same quality of work you are producing now, leaving early on Thursday would be OK. I suggest we give it a try and see how it works."

Tomas was very appreciative. He did great work for his boss and their organization. For the Hawks, at the end of the season Tomas was their Most Valuable Player.

Tomas placed a high valence on being able to leave work early one day a week because it led to an outcome he highly valued—playing for the Hawks. His boss understood this and was able to make it happen. Tomas's motivation was outstanding as was his work. No coworkers complained. They knew the boss tried to help them individually achieve the rewards each desired. Does your manager know what you want from the workplace? What your coworkers want?

This idiographic or individual nature of rewards can be lost easily. Because the office has done well, everyone gets tickets to a local professional baseball team. Well, not everyone cares about baseball or the local team. How is that going to be seen as a reward, much less affect motivation? I have seen this many times. A company provides employees rewards for jobs well done and the rewards are not really what the employees desire. The rewards even can become a joke. Managers should know what employees want—ask them, survey them.

Remember that sometimes the most valued outcomes might be intrinsic. A simple "Great job" could make someone's day. Vic Vroom has said that if he were developing expectancy theory today, he would give more thought to intrinsic rewards.[10] They are more important than many managers realize—job satisfaction, good relations with others, a feeling of accomplishment. What intrinsic rewards do you want from your job? Are you getting them? How does that affect your motivation?

The motivations of people in the workplace are different. Some people are more highly motivated than others. Not everyone necessarily wants the same outcomes from their work. Not everyone necessarily feels fairly treated, valued, and rewarded. There are many things that can affect motivation beyond what we have discussed, such as difficulties in one's personal life, health issues, anxieties, frustrations, stress, or even psychodynamic issues from one's upbringing. These are factors about which we might have no clue. Seek to understand your own motivations. Use your knowledge of motivation to try and understand the effectiveness of those for whom you work. If you are a manager, or become a manager, perhaps the insights here will make you more effective.

Part III: Groups

CHAPTER FIVE

Norms: Beware the Unwritten Rules of the Workplace

Jonas was excited about his new position. He had been invited to join the practice of the top law firm in the city. The senior partner had told him that he would be considered for partnership in a few years. Life was good. He enjoyed his work and his colleagues. Two weeks after beginning work in the new practice, the senior partner called Jonas into her office and motioned him to the window overlooking the parking lot.

"Is that your '57 Chevy out there?" questioned the senior partner.
Jonas answered, "Sure is. It's a classic. I prefer to drive it instead of garaging it."
"That's fine," replied the senior partner, "just don't drive it here and park it in our parking lot. Take a look at the other cars—Lexus, Mercedes, Cadillac. Get yourself a nice car and you'll be OK."

For these lawyers driving a car befitting their status was a group norm, an unwritten rule of behavior. If you did not drive a luxury car, you were not really part of the group; you were not projecting the image the group wanted to project. Although this might seem unreasonable, we intuitively know the reality and pervasiveness of group norms.

High schools and junior highs are notorious for cliques—geeks, jocks, goths, bandies, popular kids—each group having their own way of dressing and behaving. Norms do not disappear as we move through life. They exist in the workplace—sometimes clearly for all to see, sometimes subtle, other times hidden.

Key: Unwritten rules of behavior can affect our lives in the workplace in powerful ways; violating norms can be risky.

Norms are behavioral standards that evolve in groups and influence the behavior of group members. You violate group norms at your own risk. If you are new to the workplace and you are working harder than others around you, you might be violating a performance norm. If so, a coworker might give you a friendly hint, "Hey, slow down. You'll make us all look bad." Failure to adjust will lead to increased pressure from your coworkers and the danger of being alienated.

That's what Elto Mayo of the Harvard Business School found in research conducted at Western Electric's Hawthorne Works in Cicero, Illinois, in the late 1920s and mid-1930s—the classic Hawthorne studies. Mayo found that workers could produce more than they chose to produce. Workers informally determined a performance standard and did not let on to management that they could do more.

Workplace norms can develop about appropriate dress, speech, quality of work, quantity of work, hours expended at work, and on and on. Not every behavior in the workplace has a norm, just those that have evolved for whatever reason as being important to the group.[1] Some norms are more important than others. Sometimes a norm that has existed for a long time can transition to a rule or regulation, such as a dress code that is put in writing. Furthermore, norms vary from workplace to workplace, group to group, and situation to situation. Explicit norms usually are not hard to recognize. You are told what they are or they are readily apparent.

> Scarlett wanted to make a good impression on the first day of her new job at a major financial firm in Chicago. Office hours were 8 a.m. to 5 p.m. Scarlett got up early and was in the office by 7:30 a.m. As she walked in, her new boss snorted, "Where have you been? You're late."
>
> "I thought our hours are from eight to five?" Scarlett questioned.
>
> Her new supervisor looked at her, smiled, and said, "Yes, technically you are right but no one here works those hours. You'll find most of us here from seven to six."

Implicit norms, conversely, can be difficult to recognize. We might not even know that we have violated them until it is too late. As a young Air Force officer, I had to give a monthly presentation to a two-star general (brigadier generals are one star; major generals, two stars; lieutenant generals, three stars; generals, four stars). The first time I gave this presentation, I arrived five minutes early. My boss was waiting for me. "You're late," he said. "For one-star generals, five minutes is OK. Two stars you have to be here ten minutes early; three stars fifteen." At that Air Force base this was the norm. Now imagine that my boss had not been there to clarify this norm. Each month I would have arrived about five minutes before my presentation to the two-star general officer. What would the general's secretary have thought of me? What would his other administrative staff have thought? The young officer is disrespectful, doesn't understand how we do things, doesn't care. In short, I'd have risked creating a negative impression because of an implicit norm that I did not know existed.

Both of these examples involved time and the same behavior, "being late." In the Chicago firm, the norm was explicit and would have been easy to identify even if Sharon's boss had not pointed it out. In my Air Force story, the norm was implicit and I could have created a bad impression by my ignorance or if I had not taken my boss's counsel.

> Ethan was a little nervous. As a young analyst, he had been invited to give a presentation for the first time at a meeting of the senior management team. His presentation caused much discussion, with VPs interrupting and debating among themselves. About halfway through the presentation, there was an issue that generated extended conversation among the team at the table. Five minutes passed; then ten, as the discussion continued. Roger could see this was going to go on for a while. He moved from behind the podium where he had been standing and took a seat at the far end of the conference table away from the senior management team. After another ten minutes, they concluded their discussion.
>
> Ethan moved back to the podium and completed his presentation. The CEO thanked him and excused him from the room. After Ethan was gone, the CEO turned to the VP in Ethan's chain of command and said, "Your analyst's presentation was OK but he lacks good judgment. We don't need people in our organization who lack common sense. He had no business sitting at this table without being invited."

Ethan violated an implicit norm which he did not know existed, and it cost him his job. Really. Ethan probably never was told the real reason he lost his job, but rumors probably would have circulated in the organization about what happened. Those rumors would clarify this norm for other employees. Although Ethan's situation might seem unfair and extreme, these things happen. More likely in this situation, the CEO and others on the senior management team simply would have a less favorable view of Ethan, and this could affect his advancement and opportunities.

How could Ethan's situation have been avoided, other than there being a change in senior leadership or Ethan having a VP in his chain who would go to bat for him? Because Ethan was giving a presentation to the senior leadership team for the first time, Ethan's boss should have prepped him on what to expect, what to do, what not to do. Ethan, however, also has responsibility here. He is the one giving the presentation. Ethan should have asked his boss if there was anything he needed to know or should be aware of when giving a presentation to the senior team. Furthermore, Ethan could have checked with his peers and others who might have already had this experience. If Ethan's office had an administrative assistant or secretary who had been there for a while, the secretary might know the ropes or know a secretary for a member of the senior team who would know them. Understanding that informal norms might exist in a situation is a first step toward identifying them. The motto of the Boy Scouts and Girl Scouts, "Be prepared," is a useful guide. The more you know about a situation you are getting into, the more effectively you can perform.

> **Key: Unwritten rules apply only to behaviors—not to what you think.**

Norms are about behaviors, and are not about your feelings or your thoughts.[2] People need informal rules to be able to work together. The norms that affect us the most are those of our immediate work groups or teams, the people with whom we work and interact. Imagine the chaos if we eliminated every workplace norm from where we work. Picture an office where there are no norms for things such as dress, appropriate speech and conduct, or performance. Norms indicate what the group considers to be acceptable workplace attitudes and behaviors.

Sometimes norms extend to verbal behaviors—the things we say, the subjects we talk about, or what we do not talk about. There also might be norms about what we say in public that are different from what we say in private. As a worker making a GM or Ford car, you can think—correctly or incorrectly—that Toyota or Honda has higher overall quality. You might or might not be able to express that opinion to your fellow worker's. You might want to be careful, however, about with whom and in which situations you express this opinion.

There usually are some thoughts we have as individuals that are best left unsaid in the workplace. A group might or might not care what you actually think as long as your behavior is consistent with that of other group members. The Air Force has a rule about members not having beards. I like beards. Some of our greatest military leaders wore beards. So what's the big deal? Thinking this and discussing this was fine—as long as I did not grow a beard. I remember being an Air Force Academy cadet and watching protests against the Vietnam War. It mattered not how we as cadets felt about the war or whether we agreed with the protests on our nation's campuses. These were matters about which we could not take a public position as long as we were serving in the military.

It might seem disingenuous to think one way and then say something else. More likely it is not a matter of saying something else but rather not expressing an opinion that could be problematic. We make many decisions about what we give and do not give to the organizations of which we are a part. We have expectations about what we will give (e.g., time, effort, quality, loyalty) and what we expect (e.g., fair pay, equitable treatment, growth opportunities, job satisfaction). Each of us has an unwritten psychological contract with the organizations in which we participate, regardless of whether we have ever thought about this contract. These "compromises" between thought and deed are adjustments we make as part of that psychological contract. We can be ourselves in the workplace. We just need to understand the rules by which we play, learn, and work with others to get along and be effective.

> **Key: The nature of norms varies by group, type of organization, and level in the organization, with norms becoming stronger as you advance in an organization.**

Masculinity-femininity is an important dimension of national cultures, some organizational cultures, and often group norms. Sheryl Sandberg stated in *Lean In*, "The blunt truth is that men still run the world."[3] In the past two decades, significant numbers of women have moved into leadership positions in corporate America. In the United States, historically men—mostly Caucasian men—have dominated our organizations. They continue to do so in many organizations. Where men comprise most of the groups in organizations, the norms are more masculine. In organizations or parts of organizations where women are dominant, the norms are more feminine.

Does it matter whether a man or a woman leads an organization? Not to the bottom line. In the late 1980s, Jane Farrell (a graduate student) and I conducted a statistical analysis of all of the available research we could locate that asked this question. We used a technique called meta-analysis and examined results from studies conducted in organizations and studies from laboratories. For each study, we computed an effect size—how much of a difference did the sex of the leader make to outcomes—and then we computed an overall effect size across all studies. The results: It makes no difference to the bottom line whether the leader is a woman or a man.[4]

Even so, a disproportionate percentage of women drop out of corporate America as they near the top of the corporate ladder. Women seem to rise through organizations only so far and then look into the offices of top management from below, through the "glass ceiling." Sheryl Sandberg argued that women should "lean in," be more assertive, and take their places at corporate tables. Being aware of norms should make this easier.

The further one advances in organizations, the stronger the norms become—and they extend beyond the workday. Those who lead our organizations are available 24/7. There are social engagements, dinners, parties, plus the work that must get done, the decisions that must be made. You will entertain, you will be at these functions, you will see that our main client has a great time. When you are "on" all the time, disconnects between thought and deed are more likely to be revealed. Your actions must fit the group norms or you will not remain part of the group.

Troublesome are those workplaces where norms border on (or even embrace) sexual harassment, crude humor, and sexual innuendo. Polls vary but suggest that in the United States 40% to 90% of women in their jobs have experienced some form of sexual harassment.[5] As legally indefensible as these conditions might be, women could be reluctant to "rock the boat." A paycheck is a paycheck. The question becomes, "At what cost?" Some women endure very stressful working conditions that impact health and productivity just to keep a job. Where dysfunctional norms impact the quality of work life, management should exercise leadership and work to eliminate such norms. Changing norms can be difficult, but the costs here impact not only the individual but also the organization.

Key: Norms do not apply equally to everyone; there are exceptions.

Groups exercise influence over the behavior of their members through norms. People who follow the group norms "fit in"; those who do not risk rejection. Groups enforce conformity and tend to ostracize those who deviate.[6] Most people go along with most group norms. When the group norm and an individual's personal values conflict, that individual must make a decision.

Jack was part of a team working temporarily in the deep South in the early 1960s. One day the team stopped for lunch at a local restaurant known for its excellent barbecue. The team took a table and Jack started checking out the menu. Jack noticed the words, "We reserve the right to refuse service to anyone."

Asking his team members, Jack said, "Does that sentence mean what I think it means?" A coworker replied, "Probably so."

When the server arrived, Jack pointed to the sentence and questioned, "I noticed these words on your menu. Do you serve blacks?"

Without hesitation, she replied, "No, we don't."

Jack thought for a moment and replied, "Then you don't serve me." Turning to his coworkers, "Guys, make your own choices. I can't eat here. I'll be outside."

Where is that line for you? What will you tolerate? Not tolerate? At what point is a practice too shady? An action too questionable? This, too, is part of your unwritten psychological contract. Some norms we have no trouble in accommodating. Others could pose personal dilemmas. How do you decide? For me it is the newspaper test. I ask myself, if the action were the featured story in my hometown newspaper, or a headline in Google news, how would I feel? How would those I love feel?

So, what happens if you don't follow a norm? For most people, you will be subjected over time to increasing pressure to conform, starting with gentle persuasion ("You really ought to do this"), but growing increasingly strong ("If you don't do this, do you know what's going to happen to you?"), building to coercion ("Unless you do this, you can forget about anyone around here ever lifting a finger to help you"). When people deviate from a norm, it highlights what the norm is for others. The reaction of the group to the person who deviates also highlights the power of the group.

At some point in this process most people will simply go with the norm and all will be well with the group. A few people might try to change the norm. Although this might be possible, it has a low probability of success unless the person trying to change the norm has significant personal power, such as the ability to reward or coerce. Some people will do nothing and will be rejected by the group. But others will do nothing—and be just fine.

It seemed that Joe had worked for Kevenson's forever. Joe performed minimally but sufficiently to keep his job. Joe sometimes was late getting to work. He spent way too much time hanging around the coffee machine. His t-shirts, jeans, long hair, and earring were out of place in the professional environment where he worked. People would look at Joe, scratch their heads, and wonder, "How on earth does Ol' Joe keep his job?" But whenever there were new employees and they were learning the ropes, someone was sure to comment, "Just don't dress or act like Ol' Joe."

Joe was a house deviant, a person who violates norms but is kept around as an example of how not to act. If you have worked very many years, you have probably known a house deviant or two. Some people clarify norms simply because they do not conform to them. House deviants do not fit in, but they serve a useful role in the workplace. By their presence they make some norms more explicit.

There are others who can violate workplace norms and be unaffected. Norms might apply differently to different people in the same work group. Sometimes people with seniority—by virtue of their years in the workplace—might be exempt from certain norms that apply to others. There are some people who can just deviate from norms—and other rules—and get away with it.

The Army installation had to be relocated and merged with the operations at another location. This move would take great planning and coordination across all functions. Choosing the person to plan this action was easy: Captain Jones. Jones was brilliant. He did more in four hours than most accomplished in eight. He needed only four hours of sleep and when he wasn't sleeping, he was working. He had no family except his coworkers. Jones had a tremendous reputation for accomplishing the impossible efficiently and effectively.

Jones developed the plan and scheduled a briefing for the general responsible for the move. Jones was well-prepared. His plan was superb and he knew it. Jones began his PowerPoint presentation and was on the third slide when the general interrupted him.

"Excuse me, Captain. Are those red socks you're wearing?"

Indeed, Captain Jones was standing there in his green Army uniform wearing red socks—not the black socks required by regulation or expected by social norm. Without batting an eye, Jones looked at the general and replied, "Sir, the American taxpayer does not pay me because of the color socks I wear. They pay me because of what I can do for them, for you, and the United States Army. And that's why I'm giving this briefing instead of somebody else." At which point Captain Jones turned back to his slide and continued his briefing. The general said nothing. Indeed, the plan was superb.

Captain Jones had what Edwin Hollander called idiosyncrasy credits.[7] Jones could get away with this because he was so good at what he did. He was so superior in his work and expertise that he could deviate from norms without any pressures being applied. So how do you get idiosyncrasy credits? By making contributions to the group that the group perceives as being significant. The more others see you as being vital to the effective functioning of the group, the more credits you earn. You earn "chips" through your contributions and you cash in some of the chips when you deviate from norms. The problem is that you never know how many—if any—idiosyncratic credits you have until you violate a norm. You might think that you have made important contributions to the work group but the work group might not share that perception. Credits that allow you to deviate from norms are based on what others think—not on what you think. Even so, the possibility that we can build idiosyncrasy credits and have a measure of freedom navigating the unwritten rules of the workplace is encouraging.

Knowing how group norms influence individual behavior helps significantly in decoding the workplace. Norms often can explain why people do what they do, or how they do what they do. Additionally, the concepts of "house deviant" and "idiosyncrasy credits" help us understand how some among us ignore norms and suffer no consequences.

CHAPTER SIX

Roles: There Is More to a Job Than the Job Description

Catherine was a college professor. Her position required teaching courses, engaging in scholarly activities, and participating in service to the college. Based on her experiences as a professor at other academic institutions, Catherine had certain expectations about how she should do her job. Her department chair had his ideas about how Catherine should do her job, as did her peers—both in her department and in other departments. The academic dean and the president and other administrators had expectations. And, of course, so did the students in Catherine's courses. Some wanted a demanding and rewarding learning experience, but others wanted to just pass the course and move along. Students varied in what they expected from Catherine in and out of the classroom. Moreover, the parents of students sometimes had expectations for Catherine's performance—especially if they happened to be footing the bill. Catherine's partner also had expectations about how she did the job—which she learned when she pushed herself a little too hard or when she did not take time for more balance in her life activities.

There were many different people who had expectations about how Catherine performed her work as a college professor.

Key: People have expectations about how you do your job—and these expectations will differ.

Every position, office, and job has requirements, that is, responsibilities, duties, and tasks to be performed. These often are put in writing in job or position descriptions; but there always is more to a job than what is written in the description. Several people can have exactly the same job title and job description, but that does not mean that they do the job in the same way. Each person enacts the position held. The office of President of the United States does not change from president to president, but look at the many different ways in which people have carried out that office.

Roles are expected behaviors that are associated with specific positions. Regardless of the position you hold, there are people affected—directly or indirectly—by what you do and how you do it. Many, if not most, have expectations about how you perform your job and each most likely perceives your role somewhat differently. If you list all of the people with expectations about how you should do your job, then you have identified your role-set.[1]

Why should you care about identifying your role-set? Because people with expectations about how you should do your job usually try to communicate those expectations to you—to influence you—especially in those weeks and months right after you take a new position. Social psychologists Daniel Katz and Robert Kahn described this process in their role episode model.[2] People have ideas about how and what you should do ("expected role") and they might let you know what they expect, often a little bit at a time ("sent roles"). These "sent roles" are inputs (among various inputs) that you can accept, reject, or put on hold as you determine how you see your job ("perceived role"). As you go about doing your job ("enacted role"), your behaviors provide feedback to the people in your role-set.

> Zoey was new to her job and it seemed everyone was eager to give her advice. One day an incident with a customer occurred. It was a type of incident that she was trained to report to her supervisor. A coworker chimed in, however, telling Zoey, "I know we're supposed to inform the boss whenever this happens, but it just happens every now and then, so usually we just don't bother." Another coworker overhearing the conversation added, "The procedure manual says to report it but nobody does. If we did, it would just make our job harder."

Zoey's coworkers were communicating their expectations about how Zoey was to do her job. Except for those to whom you directly report, these comments usually just come up in casual conversation or as an aside ("Oh, by the way. . . ."). If your antennae are not up, you could easily miss or dismiss them. But these "tidbits" can be useful information. They vary and even might be contradictory, but the information provides insight about what others expect of you and of potential sources of conflict.

So do you go along with these expectations? That's up to you. Most likely you will find some to be beneficial and some not. Sometimes people will "back off," and adjust their expectations. Other times they might increase their attempts to influence you. Through your actions you send messages about how you see your role. In response to your actions, others send you messages about how they see your role. Being aware of this ongoing process, recognizing these communications, understanding the significance of your actions in the eyes of others—these all make you more knowledgeable about what is going on around you, and help you to decode the workplace.

Within an organization you might have several roles. Your primary organizational role is associated with your formal office or position, but you might enact other roles. You could have other formal roles associated with other work groups, such as committees, task forces, or process-improvement teams. In addition to the formal relationships in organizations, there are informal relationships. These informal groups also have roles—such as the informal leader whose opinion is highly valued by coworkers.

By the time we enter the workforce, most of us are pretty experienced at taking on roles, both organizationally and socially. We learn how to be a student, a club member, a soccer player, a band member, a gang member, and so on. From our earliest years, we also learn roles associated with our sex—how to be a boy, a girl, a man, a woman. These sex roles—which affect significant aspects of our behavior across social settings—impact the workplace.

> **Key: Most people, regardless of whether they realize it, have stereotypic expectations about how men and women should act.**

Understanding the importance of organizational roles and the role episode model can be empowering. It enables us to decode what is happening around us and respond accordingly. Understanding sex roles in the workplace is different. Sex-role stereotyping is pervasive. Intentionally or not, we see the workplace through a lens of masculinity-femininity. Our own perception of appropriate sex-typed behaviors can affect how we enact organizational roles. Our perception of organizational role behaviors that we value and reward also could be sex biased.[3] Such perceptions of appropriate and inappropriate sex roles can be a disadvantage to organizational members and the organization.

Read the following words and ask yourself which you think are more likely to describe men? Which are more likely to describe women?

Aggressive, works well with others, dynamic, good administrator, logical, perceptive, assertive, personable, forceful, tactful, true leader. For years I have used a longer version of this exercise in the classroom. Consistently most of my students see these words as either masculine or feminine.

The effect of our masculinity-femininity lens can be subtle, easily missed, yet significant in impact. A supervisor can be fair in treatment, actively promote equal opportunity, and still manifest stereotypic tendencies without being aware of it. How? One example is performance appraisals. Analyses of key words such as those listed above found in written performance appraisals sometimes show sex-role stereotypic traits. A male manager is described as "a true leader," "dynamic," "logical," "assertive," or "forceful." A female manager—viewed as equally effective—might be described as "a good administrator," "works well with others," "perceptive," "personable," or "tactful." Somewhere from within us, the masculine and feminine traits we have learned from our childhood emerge in our writing and in our speech, unintentionally affecting opportunities.

Consider leadership. Years ago *Fortune* had an issue that listed "America's Toughest Bosses." Why "toughest"? Why not "most effective" or "most successful"? In *The Human Equation,* Jeffrey Pfeffer of the Stanford Graduate School of Business suggested that, in America, there is a perception that "good managers are mean or tough" even though there is little evidence to support that contention.[4] Good managers from CEOs to first-line supervisors show a wide range of behaviors and styles.

In the 1920s, Mary Follett wrote about the assumption that "you cannot be a good leader unless you are aggressive, masterful, dominating." She argued, "I think, not only that these characteristics are not the qualities essential to leadership, but, on the contrary, that they often militate directly against leadership."[5] Nearly a century later, many of us still think good leaders must be aggressive and dominant, characteristics people tend to associate more with men than women. With a few exceptions, such as nursing and teaching, "a good manager is still perceived as predominantly masculine."[6]

The reorganization was going to be challenging to say the least. Frank had to appoint someone to lead the effort. In his office with several senior officials, Frank asked for input.

"Frank, I think Bob Lewis would do a great job here. I think he's ready for a big challenge. Let's see what he can do," said Harry.

Steve replied, "Bob would probably do a good job but I think we ought to give Jane Kanady the job. Jane's doing great work for us and showing real

> leadership. Plus we need to give our senior women more opportunities like this one."
> Frank thought for a moment and then said," Steve, I agree with you about Jane and giving our women more opportunities—but this is a man's job. I'm going with Bob Lewis. There will be other opportunities for Jane."

Variations on this theme play out behind closed doors, contributing to the "glass ceiling" that women face. In *Men and Women of the Corporation,* Rosabeth Moss Kanter referred to the role encapsulation of women and other minorities.[7] Women could be encapsulated; that is, given positions perceived as appropriate for women, positions that might be marginalized and be less rewarded by the organization. It should be noted, however, that some women prefer jobs perceived as "women's jobs." We perceive certain jobs as more for men—such as being mechanic or construction worker—and other jobs as more for women—such as being an elementary school teacher or social worker. Consequently, corporate programs that use an affirmative-action approach to move women into non-traditional jobs will be popular with some but not all. Strategies that encourage equal opportunity for all positions could find a disproportionate number of women still seeking "women's jobs," such as those in human resources, personnel, or administration.

You will see examples of sex-role stereotyping in the workplace. Try to be aware of your own sex-role stereotyping, subtle though it could be. Also be aware that others might see you through their sex-role stereotypic lens.

Key: Roles are major sources of stress in our lives.

Who are you? One of my first research studies years ago at the United States Air Force Academy posed this question to my classmates. Most gave answers such as "cadet," "brother," "son," "friend," "athlete," and "pilot." All of these are roles. We all have multiple roles—our organizational roles, social roles, and family roles. A great source of stress comes from conflicts among these roles, conflicts that we sometimes cannot resolve.[8]

The soccer game for the league championship was to begin at 6:00 p.m. Teresa's nine-year-old daughter would be playing. Teresa had promised to be there; besides, she did not want to miss it. At 3:00 p.m. Teresa's boss informed her that the agenda for the meeting tomorrow had been changed.

Teresa needed to finish her report so that her boss could review the numbers before the 9:00 a.m. meeting.

"Finish the report?" she thought, "I have hours of work left to do. If I don't have it ready for the meeting, life could get pretty hard around here. But if I finish the report, I'm going to miss my daughter's game—and I promised."

Teresa had interrole conflict. How can she be a good mother and a good employee? There is only so much time in a day. I can remember a time in my life when I had to put in some extra long hours on the job for a while. I made a point of being home by 6 p.m. to be with my family but I was back in the office by 8 p.m. I remember patting myself on the back because at least I went home. My coworkers still were plugging away. Today I think about where I put my energies back then and I just scratch my head. There are no easy answers. There is only so much time and energy. Few of us can do it all.

Sometimes we get conflicting messages or expectations from the same person. On Monday the boss tells you how she wants something done. On Wednesday she changes her mind, and tells you that she wants it done a different way. On Friday, she has thought about it and decided that the approach she suggested on Monday was probably the way to go, after all. For some supervisors and their employees, this intransender role conflict is a way of life. Intersender role conflict occurs when conflicting or incompatible expectations come from different members of your role-set.

Tom could retire but he thought the opportunity to work directly for Mr. Barrows would be worth staying for a few more years, plus Chicago was a great city. Mr. Barrows was known throughout the corporation for his innovation and being able to make things happen. After assuming his new job, Tom realized that much of his day-to-day work would not be with Mr. Barrows, to whom he reported, but rather with Mr. Davis. Mr. Davis was at the same level in the corporation as Mr. Barrows and had just as much power.

Unfortunately for Tom, Mr. Barrows and Mr. Davis did not get along. In fact they hated each other. Everything Tom did for Mr. Davis, Mr. Barrows disapproved of and vice versa. After a few weeks of this Tom questioned his decision to work there. After he broke out in hives, Tom realized that he had had enough. Tom quit the job he had so looked forward to and retired to the sunny skies and beaches of southern California.

Tom clearly had intersender role conflict. The stress from this conflict caused health issues and consequently changed his retirement plans.

Kerri knew that there was only one way to do what the company wanted him to do—but doing it was against everything he had been taught since he was a kid. It wasn't illegal but it was unethical, and it made Kerri feel very uncomfortable just thinking about it.

Kerri had person-role conflict. His personal values conflicted with the expectations of his role-set. In our unwritten psychological contract there are performance expectations which we agree to without hesitation. They are reasonable, appropriate, and acceptable. But we can encounter expectations that we deem unreasonable, highly inappropriate, and unacceptable—lines we will not cross. In between is a gray area. We each discern the acceptable and unacceptable lines. It is the decisions that fall into the gray area that are problematic, and where we must come to our own decisions.

> Nanji would be a college junior in the fall, but she was excited to be a summer intern at a major company in her hometown. During the first few days she was kept busy learning about the workplace. After that things got hazy. She was supposed to be an administrative assistant but she wasn't really sure what that job entailed. Her immediate supervisor went on vacation and when he returned he had a business trip. Occasionally people would give her things to do but often she had no idea how she was to do them or even whom to ask. As the summer passed, Nanji grew disillusioned. No one ever had time for her. She was never sure what she was hired to do.

Nanji never figured out her role. Not knowing what is expected from one's role-set also can be stressful. How do you know what to do or if you are doing it properly? People in such situations might think, "Am I supposed to be doing something I don't know about? What does my boss really expect me to be doing?" A written job description might be given, but in the absence of communicated expectations and feedback, role ambiguity can make life difficult. In one study, George Graen reported that 80% of administrative assistants in a service organization did not know "what the supervisor wanted" even though they had been in their jobs for more than nine months.[9]

Sometimes we can take on so many roles that we experience role overload, we just can't do everything we need to do. Over time, most of us learn to say "no." As a professor, there always is another committee, another ad hoc task force, another position in faculty governance or a professional organization asking for my service. When you have a choice, sometimes "no" is the best answer.

To decode the workplace, you must understand the pervasiveness of roles, both organizational and societal, and their impact. You inhabit multiple roles. Everyone with whom you work inhabits multiple roles. Listen and you will hear people communicating expectations about roles. Listen and you will hear people dealing with the stress that grows out of role conflicts.

Organizational Socialization: New Employees Act Differently Than Current Employees

Calida was excited about her new position because it came with significant responsibility and opportunity for advancement. After her newcomer's orientation to the organization and meetings with senior officials, Calida was highly motivated and ready to go. Then she met with her immediate supervisor and was shown her office. Calida was surprised—no one had cleaned the office. An empty bag of potato chips lay on the floor, along with a few paper clips, folders, and crumpled papers. A film of dust covered the furniture suggesting that the room had been vacant for some time. The old, gray desk was piled high with papers and miscellaneous trash. The drawers were cluttered with material left behind by the previous occupant. Calida would spend the better part of a day just making her office livable.

The implicit message Calida received was clear—we don't really care about you—and, as Calida was to learn, the company didn't. The people were nice enough, but the organization itself had no concept of the value people make to the bottom line.

Think for a moment about jobs you have had. How were you welcomed to that job? Think about that first day. What was it like? Pleasant? Unpleasant? Exciting? Scary? Consider the first several days; the first few weeks; the first few months. How long did it take you to feel comfortable in your new position? How easy was it for you to learn the norms and roles, to learn the ropes? How easy was it for you to learn what it took to get the job done, get ahead, and stay out of trouble? How much help did you get from the organization for which you worked? What about from your supervisor? Did your coworkers help? Could your transition to the new job have been made easier? Better? How?

For many of us, our transitions to new jobs could have been much better. If we are fortunate, we might get an orientation to the company and an overview of the job and workplace from our supervisor. Usually we learn the important norms and roles of the workplace through trial and error. These trials and errors can be costly, however, both to the individual and the organization.

Companies vary in how effective they are at welcoming the new employee but most could use an overhaul. Managers fail to recognize that the behavior of the new employee is different from the behavior of employees who have been with the organization a while. The new employee is looking for information, trying to fit in. For the organization, this is an opportunity that too often is lost.

When we are new to an organization we try to learn the norms, roles, and values associated with our new position. This process is called "organizational socialization." It actually starts in earlier years as we pick up bits and pieces of information about different jobs, occupations, and professions.

> **Key: No matter how much we learn about a new job, career, or organization before making a change, there always will be aspects—often important ones—that we do not know about.**

As a young boy I watched Air Force B-52 jet bombers flying high over the Piedmont of North Carolina, their white contrails unfolding as they traveled to the mountains of western North Carolina to practice bombing. They flew very high; they were just specks in the sky. I watched also as they returned, traversing the sky eastward. I wondered what it was like up there. What would it be like to fly such a plane; to see the earth far below?

I saw the movie "X-15" five times. My dad would take me to our local airport and sometimes he would find a pilot to give us a flight over our hometown in a small Cessna for $10. We enjoyed looking at the world below. I watched the pilot fly the Cessna. I devoured every book I could find about pilots and planes and pilot training. I wanted to learn to fly, to be an Air Force pilot.

Eventually I was very fortunate and awarded a congressional appointment to the United States Air Force Academy near Colorado Springs,

Colorado. There the socialization was intense. We viewed film after film showing combat flying. We met pilots. We flew in high-performance aircraft. Flying upside down at 40,000 feet, I looked up at the earth. I traveled faster than the speed of sound. After the Academy I went to Georgia for Undergraduate Pilot Training. My classmates chose a patch that I designed for our class—a flying fetus wearing a pilot's helmet and oxygen mask, with the words, "Born to Fly."

Even with all of my initial socialization and motivation, however, I grew to recognize a gap between me and the norms and roles of the fighter pilot. This only became clear to me during Undergraduate Pilot Training. The Air Force was teaching me to be a military aviator but it just was not me. I realized that, although I loved flying, being a military aviator—and everything that job entails—just wasn't a good fit for me. Among other things, I realized how much of my time I would be spending with my flying squadron and how little time I would be spending with my bride-to-be, and hopefully someday a family. For me, the thrill of flying high and fast was not enough to sustain a commitment to pursue a career as an Air Force aviator. God bless those who do have that commitment, for our nation needs them. I chose to serve our nation and the Air Force in other ways. I left the Air Force pilot training program and earned a private pilot's license on my own. In spite of my high motivation, reading, studying, conversations, and flying experiences, my knowledge of what it took to be an Air Force aviator was limited. You never can be fully prepared for what an occupation, career, or organization really is like.

> Jennifer knew that she was ready for a career in a Big Four accounting firm. She completed her degree at the top of her class. Great things were expected from her and she knew it. Recruiters wanted her and the bidding for her was fierce. When the dust settled, she took a position with her first choice of the Big Four accounting firms.
>
> Within days Jennifer was crunching numbers and analyzing data the way the company wanted it done. Unfortunately that work pattern did not change. She was working 12-hour days, traveling much, but doing the same thing over and over. No creativity. No chance to use her mind. This was not what Jennifer had anticipated. Sure, the pay was great but who had time to enjoy it? And where was the challenging work she had been led to expect.
>
> Jennifer discussed this with her mentor only to be told this is the way it will be for the first five years, until she had enough seniority and experience to lead her own team. Her dream job was not at all what she had expected. After two years, Jennifer had had enough; she resigned.

What Jennifer thought her job would be like and the reality of her job did not match. We learn about what organizations and jobs can be like from many sources, such as friends, neighbors, the Internet, even on TV and in movies. Some things might be accurate but other things are not. I once asked a student from Africa what he thought of the United States; his answer surprised me. "I am amazed by how hard Americans work," he replied, "Not at all like the American television programs I watched back home."

> **Key: Organizational socialization occurs in training, education, apprenticeships, and even selection methods.**

We are socialized into organizations in different ways. Some methods are planned but most are informal and unplanned. During training we are being socialized. Instructors express values; these values are clarified and reinforced in interactions with those being trained. As a young officer learning to fly military aircraft, I was learning much more than how to fly planes. I was learning the culture and subcultures of Air Force pilots. Many of the pilots who trained us were seasoned in the skies of Vietnam; their stories prepared us for combat. The learning was not found in textbooks but rather in the interactions and the attitudes expressed.

Education plays a formidable role in our socialization, starting when we are young. Our education system emphasizes student learning and evaluates the individual student and yet, when we arrive in the workplace, we find that groups and teams are the real building blocks of our organizations and—formally and informally—we must work together to achieve the objectives of the organization. Colleges and universities are very much institutions of socialization. A college graduate tends to have more in common with another college graduate than with a high school graduate.

At the highest academic levels the socialization process can be intense. You might have heard it said that earning a PhD is like joining a club. Your doctoral committee and other professors are sizing you up to determine whether you should be allowed to join their ranks.

When I was a graduate student, I perceived clear role expectations as to how to be a "good" graduate student. On the first day of the term, a professor held a meeting of the new students and said, "If you are wondering how to act, how to survive, how to get through this, then just act like Kay. She's been here two years and is the model graduate student." We were given a specific example, a person to observe, a person whom to ask questions. Understanding our roles as graduate students was important.

To be admitted to doctoral candidacy, each student had to meet with a committee of professors. The professors can ask any questions they think appropriate to test the student's knowledge. Any subject matter in the discipline is fair game. Students at my university had to pass these examinations to change their status from doctoral students to doctoral candidates. Once they were doctoral candidates, the students could begin researching and writing their dissertations.

Going into my exam I was terrified and subservient, which coincidently happened to be the proper graduate student role in this case. Fortunately I passed. Another graduate student figured that if Ballard could pass, how hard could it really be? From my perspective this was a reasonable assumption. Unfortunately, this student did not fully grasp the importance of the graduate student role, especially in this situation. She arrived at her exam very confident with a plate full of freshly baked cookies for the committee to enjoy. Her questions were much tougher than mine had been, very challenging, nearly impossible, or so it seemed. She had not played the role. She did not pass until her second try at the exam a few months later.

This socialization into occupations, jobs, and professions is a by-product of our learning new knowledge, skills, and abilities. A friend of mine is a carpenter. Joking with me, he once said that if I ever found myself out of work, he could take me on as an apprentice. He obviously had never seen me drive a nail. I am sure, however, that if I were his apprentice I would learn far more than carpentry. I would learn what carpenters think of electricians, plumbers, suppliers, contractors, and others in the industry.

Some organizations—and people—shape socialization processes through their methods of selecting new employees. There are many stories about how Admiral Hyman Rickover chose officers to join his team. Admiral Rickover is the "father of the nuclear navy" and mentored Jimmy Carter when Carter was a young naval officer. In an eulogy after his father's passing, Robert Rickover noted that the interviews his father conducted with officers were "legendary"; that his father "wanted to make sure they could adapt to whatever situation they found themselves in, and so they were often placed in unexpected and stressful circumstances."[1] The following story has been told in many ways.[2]

Admiral Rickover put out the word that he was looking for some officers for a new endeavor. Ensign Thomas wanted the challenge and opportunity that always came with working for this great man. Ensign Thomas went to meet the admiral. He was told to go on into the admiral's spacious office where he found Admiral Rickover at his desk reviewing some papers.

Saluting sharply, he stated, "Sir, I am Ensign Thomas. I understand you are looking for a few good officers. Sir, I would like to join your team."

Without even looking up, Admiral Rickover said in a matter-of-fact voice, "Make me mad."

Ensign Thomas pondered very briefly. He could take orders. The admiral said to make him mad. Sitting on the admiral's desk was an exquisite "ship in a bottle." With one quick swoop of his arm, Thomas grabbed the ship in a bottle and flung it violently against the wall—WHAM—smashing it into a thousand pieces.

Admiral Rickover looked up at Ensign Thomas, stared him in the face, and said simply, "You're hired."

I often have wondered if the admiral kept a closet full of ships in bottles—or models of the Nautilus submarine, which is sometimes used in a different version of this tale. Such stories become larger than life, changing and becoming more embellished over time. These stories, however, illustrate how a selection method can be pivotal in organizational socialization. Look at the characteristics of the work team Rickover would get with this method: officers who could think on their feet, who could take orders, and who were not afraid to take risks and live with the consequences. Why do some organizations take months to hire a person and use multiple selection methods? Many are looking for people who fit the organization's culture, people who will assimilate more quickly into its workforce—people who have "the right stuff" for that organization.

> **Key: Organizations, supervisors, and coworkers vary significantly in how much they help new employees "learn the ropes."**

We most frequently associate organizational socialization with the new employee, but organizational socialization also occurs whenever a person moves to a new position within the same company. Each new position brings a new role-set and new group norms. Ed Schein has suggested that people are most susceptible to the normative influence of others right before changing to a new position and just after the change.[3] Even before assuming a new job, often the person moving to a new position tries to learn as much as possible about that job. One way is to talk to other people who might be able to share insights and information about the job. People changing positions often try to reduce the number of surprises that they might encounter that first day or first week in the new job.

> Jeff was excited to be in his first white-collar office job. To look the part, Jeff bought several expensive sports coats, slacks, and sharp ties. He was ready. On the first day at the new job, Jeff came to work early and watched his coworkers arrive in business-casual attire, not in sports coats and colorful ties—and no suits. As dressed, Jeff did not fit in.

As discussed, we live in a perceptual world. In most organizations, how others see you—regardless of whether they tell you—makes and breaks careers, opens doors, and also denies opportunities. The more information you can get about a job beforehand, the better prepared you will be, but most of the learning about the norms, roles, and values of the organization occur after you start the job.

Organizational socialization cannot be avoided. When you take a new job or position, you must figure out what to do and how to do it. People vary in how quickly they learn workplace norms, role expectations, and the culture of the workplace. People who quickly pick up on these aspects of the work situation have an advantage. Those who do not might struggle with trying to determine how to fit in. Research suggests that good organizational socialization helps employees to be productive sooner.[4]

The quality of those first few days and weeks in a new job or new organization set the stage for all that follows. If you have a good experience right from the start, you form positive impressions that often can affect both your satisfaction with your job and your commitment to the organization.

> Elizabeth Campbell had just graduated from college and accepted an entry-level position with Onoco. She had heard Onoco was a good place to work. Now it was her first day on the job; she arrived at her office cubicle not knowing what to expect. There on her desk was a coffee mug. On one side it read, "Onoco: Caring for your tomorrow today," and on the other side it read simply, "Liz Campbell." "They know I prefer to be called 'Liz,'" she thought.
>
> Just then her new boss walked in. "We are happy to have you with us, Liz." Pointing to the mug, he said, "Not sure if you drink coffee or tea. Just a small token to say welcome to our team. Let me show you around—and if you'd like a hot beverage, bring your mug. Coffee and tea are right down the hall and to the right."
>
> Liz thought, "I just might like this place." And she did.

How would you feel if you arrived at your first day on the job and a mug was sitting on your desk personalized with your name on it? For most of us it would be a nice start. As a token, the mug conveys the message "You're valued," "We care about you," "You are one of us now." But if Liz's boss did not value people and his other actions were inconsistent with this gesture, the mug would have been hypocritical. If "mugs for newbies" had been a company policy but was not seen as important by managers, then any gains would be minimal. If "mugs for newbies" is consistent with the supervisor's management style, however, then such a small welcoming gesture could pay dividends.

Some companies have formal assimilation programs to help people understand the organization, learn personnel policies, and become informed on available benefits. There might be orientations or training. Other organizations have little or no such programs. My hunch is that organizations that view people as assets—and less so as costs—are more likely to have fully developed socialization efforts across different levels within the organization.

Usually, these formal socialization efforts do not occur at the workplace level. What happens in the workplace more likely varies from supervisor to supervisor. Over the years I learned from my own experiences—both the good and the not so good. Eventually I understood the value of facilitating the transition of the new employees who worked for me. I did the formal stuff, such as our mission, goals, who's who, policies, and expectations, but I also tried to affect the informal. Supervisors often assign someone to help a new employee learn the ropes. Who gets that job? In many cases it is the person who has the time, or can take the time, to show the newbie around and answer questions as they arise. So who has the time? It usually is not your top performers because they are too busy. Their time is much too valuable for such activities. So we turn over the socialization of the new employee to a current employee who might not be the best role model. Is this really what we want to do?

"Perry, we've got that new hire coming in next week in your section. I'd like Rasheed to show him around, help him learn the ropes."
"You know Rasheed's our best worker. He's up to his waist in alligators already."
"I know, but you know how I feel about bringing the new folks on properly. A little investment now will pay off for us later. It usually does. Cut Rasheed just a little slack. Be sure he understands how important this is."
"We'll make it happen."

New employees are going to learn from their interactions with others. Who best for those first interactions than those employees who model the values and attitudes you want to foster in your organization.

> **Key: Ultimately much of what you learn about surviving and succeeding in the organization is from "trial and error."**

We often overlook the fact that the behavior of a new employee is different and is going to be different for a while. When you are new to an organization, you really are trying to figure out how to act. If you are not doing this, then you really could be setting yourself up for difficulties. Most of us are trying to fit in, even if we are not conscious of it. We are social animals; we want to get along with others.

People will communicate norm and role expectations to you. Some of these communications will be clear; others will not. If you pick up on these communications, they can help you formulate your own hypotheses about what is going on around you and help you decode the workplace. Listen, observe, and learn. So what is expected of me? By my boss? By my coworkers? By subordinates? How do I stay out of trouble? How do I get ahead? Who's getting the rewards? Who's not? Why? Most people who have been there for a while already have their own answers to such questions. It doesn't mean that they necessarily have the right answers, but they have moved on and their behavior is different from yours.

Much of the learning of the new workplace is trial and error. We get ideas by watching and listening to others. We determine how accurate those ideas are through our experiences in the new workplace.

Sam liked his new job. It offered opportunities and benefits that were much better than those of his previous company, a small family-owned business. The second week on the job, several of his coworkers invited him out to lunch at a nearby eating establishment. They were seated and the server arrived promptly.

"Good afternoon. My name is Sarveto. May I take your drink orders?"
Sam replied, "I'll have a Heineken." The orders continued around the table.
"Diet Pepsi."
"Iced tea please."
"Just water with lemon for me."
"I'll have a Coke with lots of ice."

After the drinks arrived, it hit Sam: He was the only one who had ordered
an alcoholic beverage. At his old job, he and his boss had lunch together
several times a week and always had a cold beer.

"I notice I'm the only one with a beer. Anything I need to know?"

"The company frowns on drinking at lunch. Something about image. Not
policy—just something we tend not to do."

This possibility had never occurred to Sam; it wasn't part of his experience.
Now he knew. At least he had the good sense to ask.

We bring to every new position our own life and work experiences. These
experiences frame our perceptions, filter what we see, give meaning to
what we observe, help us process the expectations of others, help us determine how to act. Some things we did elsewhere might be fine; others
might be inappropriate.

When I arrived at Mount St. Joseph University in Cincinnati, Ohio, I
was not "tabula rasa," a "blank slate." Rather, I brought with me the experiences of having been a professor at other institutions of higher learning. I
had my own template of how to enact the role of professor. I had my own
template to help identify salient norms. My previous experiences gave me
hypotheses about how to act, how to fit in. But those hypotheses had to
be tested with the data of my new workplace. Part of successfully adapting
to a new workplace is recognizing any adjustments we need to make to fit
in and work effectively. Even CEOs need to make such adjustments to be
effective.

Courtney Hertza was a newly minted PhD from a top research university.
She applied for academic positions at several universities that—like her
alma mater—emphasized research, not teaching. The position that she was
offered and that she accepted, however, was at a small liberal arts college.

That first year, Courtney tried to continue her research agenda but the
heavy teaching load made it difficult—something had to give. From her
experience, Courtney knew the importance of research and publishing
in the best journals. She chose to put less effort into the classroom and
more into her research. The results were reflected in course evaluations
completed by her students. Unfortunately for Courtney, her liberal arts college—although encouraging research—valued teaching above all.

Courtney brought to her new position her own expectations about
being a professor that were based on professors at the research university
where she had been educated. If she did notice that expectations for the
professors at her liberal arts college were different, then she failed to act on
that knowledge. She did not adjust to her new workplace environment.

Previous experiences provide ideas as to how we should act; however, we should check those ideas with what we learn about the new workplace.

> **Key: As you experience a new workplace, you create a psychological contract with the organization—a contract with costs and benefits as you see them.**

Each of us develops a psychological contract during the first weeks and months in a new job. We have expectations about what we are willing to give an organization and what we expect in return. Some of these expectations are upfront and perhaps negotiated during the hiring or promotion process, such as salary, medical benefits, vacation, and childcare. Others are implicit and based on the templates from our previous experiences or evolve during the first weeks and months on the job. For example, what level of effort do you put into your work?

> Everyone in the office marveled at Karen. If there were a superwoman, she was it. She got the toughest assignments and made them look easy. Admired by all, praised by her bosses, Karen was a wonder. Her coworkers were amazed how anyone could work so hard all of the time.
>
> Karen knew how others viewed her and thought, "If they only knew." She was a hard worker, a smart worker, with outstanding organizing skills. Although occasionally an assignment would cause her to turn up her effort, most of the time she was on cruise control with plenty of energy to spare. She thought, "If I worked as hard as I could, they really would be amazed."

Do you give 100% on the job all the time? My guess is that, if you do, you're on your way to burnout. People work at different levels of effort. Some people give so much at the office there is nothing left when they get home. Others moderate their efforts so that the jobs get done but there also is energy for other activities after work. Many of us find a happy medium that satisfies our employer and ourselves. Few people give it all each and every day.

Part of that evolving psychological contract is how hard we will work. We adjust that contract based on how we perceive the rewards. Usually we are the ones who best understand our level of effort. Others see the results, but don't necessarily see what it took to achieve those results.

So, am I advocating coasting in our jobs? Of course not. The new employee especially must work very hard initially to learn the ropes and get established. But, over time, that employee settles into a level of effort consistent with what's needed to get the job done and individual factors, such as one's need to achieve. This level varies for each person, the job, and the situational factors of the job. If you give your very best each and every moment of every day, however, then there will be nothing in reserve for when it is needed. There are times when we "turn it on" and other times when we work less hard. Employers who push employees relentlessly likely will pay the price in stress-related medical costs and absenteeism.

Another part of the psychological contract is the degree to which you "buy into" the organization's values and culture. On one end of a continuum is the organization man, described by William Whyte in the 1950s.[5] Some people commit totally to the company and conform unquestioningly to its culture, norms, and roles. On the other end of the continuum is the rebel—the person who conforms just enough to keep the job but doesn't really buy into the company's culture. The organization person attends every social function, and participates in voluntary activities as requested. The rebel attends no social functions and never does anything that is not absolutely necessary. Most of us fall somewhere in between the two ends of the spectrum. We buy into certain parts of the company culture but not others. We decide we will attend the company picnic this year but not every year. We will lead the United Fund campaign once but then that's it for voluntary activities for a while.

People differ in what they want from the organization and what they are willing to give. People differ in what memberships in organizations cost them personally, such as time, energy, and how they see the offsetting benefits. Sometimes we really do not know another person's costs or benefits.

Xavier Rodera was an outstanding pitcher for his college baseball team. He led his team to the College World Series and was a national leader in strikeouts. On draft day for professional baseball, he knew he would go high. The only question was which team would acquire rights to him. He went fifth in the draft to the Blue Stockings. The Blue Stockings made an incredibly generous offer with a fine signing bonus. To his agent's surprise, Xavier hesitated.

"Xavier, what's the matter with you? We have everything we could possibly ask for in this offer. What are you waiting for?"

"It's the hair policy, man. The Blue Stockings want short hair. It's that 'no long hair' thing, man. I like my hair. It's me."

Xavier's agent didn't get it. "What's the big deal when we are talking this kind of money? The kid's crazy," he thought. Nevertheless he tried to negotiate so Xavier could keep the long hair but he was unsuccessful.

Eventually Xavier relented and signed with the Blue Stockings. He cut his hair and revealed a gang symbol carved on the back of his neck; it had been part of a gang initiation during his youth.

The cost to Xavier was high but the benefits were great. We all pay costs to the organizations to which we belong. We give time, effort, and ideas. We receive benefits, both extrinsic and intrinsic. You have a psychological contract with every organization of which you are a part. It will be modified with time and experience. The essential framework for your psychological contract, however, was shaped in those first few months in the organization as you observed and learned, during organizational socialization.

Organizational socialization is one of the most important learning experiences in our work lives, yet it often is given little thought. It just happens. Understand that your behavior in a new position will be different. Know that the behaviors of new employees around you will be different. Be aware of how your organization facilitates these transitions or fails to facilitate them. Knowledge of organizational socialization will help you decode the workplace.

Part IV: Organization

CHAPTER EIGHT

Groups, Teams, and Organization Structure: When Your Team Should Not Be a Team

It was Megan's first day on the job. She was sitting in the office of her boss, the office manager.

"Megan, welcome aboard. You will be handling the Barklex account. Barklex has been doing business with us for many years, so I don't foresee any problems. I think Barklex is a good account to get your feet wet, to learn the basics of how we do things here. If you need any help at all, see me or ask another member of the team. We are one big family. We want everyone to be successful. If you do a good job on the Barklex account, then the team wins and that's what we want. Any questions?"

"No, sir, not yet. I'm ready to get started."

"Great. Let's walk around the office and I'll introduce you to the other members of our team."

Megan's boss used the term "team" in welcoming Megan to the work group to which she had been assigned. Teams are very popular in organizations. You might be part of a team or could be assigned to a team. Organizations want "team players," people who listen to others, work well with others, and put the team's objectives first. But just because you are put on a team, or your work group is referred to as a team, does not mean that it really is a team.

> **Key: Not all groups in the workplace that are called teams actually are teams; many are just work groups.**

Know whether you are actually part of a team or part of a work group. Managers and organizations talk a lot about teams and building teams. If pressed to define what a team is, many people might have difficulty. There are differences between work groups and teams. These differences do not seem to be common knowledge, although the differences can be very important. Knowing the difference affects both how you do your job and the things for which you are accountable.

In the *Harvard Business Review* in 1991, Katzenbach and Smith explained the difference.[1] Work groups usually have a designated leader, a person with "legitimate" authority. That authority is given to the leadership position by the organization. Megan is part of a work group. Her boss ultimately is responsible for all of the accounts managed by the people in the office. In work groups each individual is accountable for the duties required in the position. Megan alone has accountability for the Barklex account. In teams people have individual responsibilities but ultimately it is the team as a whole that is accountable. In work groups people work individually or perhaps in small groups, but typically the products are attributed to an individual, or perhaps a group of individuals. Teams work to produce team outcomes and team products. A team succeeds or fails together. Teams are highly interactive, working together toward a common purpose. Megan is part of a work group, not a team.

It is possible to be part of a work group but also have other duties as part of a team, such as being assigned (or volunteering) to serve on an ad hoc or temporary team or committee. Teams composed of representatives from different parts of an organization—different functions—might be created to resolve problems or find ways to improve cross-functional processes. These teams, rather than the individuals, are accountable for outcomes.

Even though work groups are the true building blocks of organizations, you might be in an organization that talks "teams," or calls work groups "teams." You could be involved in team-building activities, some of which could be designed to help you in your work group. You might be involved in a team-building activity, for example, in which you are asked to close your eyes and fall backward, allowing a coworker to catch you. The purpose is to help you learn to trust your coworkers and thereby strengthen team relationships. You might be in an organization that organizes employees into teams and not work groups. Perhaps your organization thinks that teams are more effective, or maybe it found that to be the case from experience. The best teams are highly interactive with members mutually supporting each other to accomplish team objectives.

Teams might be more effective in your organization, but research suggests that teams are not necessarily more effective than work groups. In 2004, Natalie Allen and Tracy Hecht summed up the research on teams.

> Although advocates of teamwork suggest that teams enhance performance, empirical evidence does not consistently, or robustly, support these claims. . . . Teams are not as effective as many believe them to be. . . . When juxtaposed, *faith* in team effectiveness among managers, employees and the general population and the *research evidence* regarding team effectiveness appear to be out of balance.[2]

Allen and Hecht suggested that organizations create teams when they are not needed, and when work groups probably are more effective.

> Rob enjoyed his work in the bank. He worked behind the scenes on investment accounts. His job included a range of activities, from evaluating opportunities to answering questions from officials who worked directly with bank clients. He was one of ten employees in his department who did this.
>
> All was well until the meeting at which Mr. Jordan made the announcement, "We have decided to reorganize all of our departments into teams. You will have training as we move to this new structure. We believe it will be more effective. I think you will find it more satisfying."
>
> The department was reorganized. All investment research now had to be discussed and agreed on by the ten-member Investment Team, including answers to questions from banking officials. The results were predictable. Response times to answer questions were longer. Much time was spent discussing investment research strategies and options and coming to a consensus. An effective work group that talked and supported each other became an ineffective team. None of the members of the old work group liked the change. To them it simply made no sense.
>
> Rob no longer enjoyed his job. He started inquiring about positions at other banks, banks that did not organize using teams.

This is not a unique situation. Organizations implement teams because they have heard teams are better. They might not actually know the best places to use teams. This is in part because we, as educators, have not done a good job teaching leaders the basics of organization design.[3] Changing an organization's structure is one of the few levers that leaders have available.[4] Unfortunately, organizational changes are not necessarily smart design choices. To understand where to use teams, you need to understand a little about organization structure. This also will help you decode your workplace.

Key: How your organization is structured affects how you do your job; organizations have different structures based on how work is grouped and coordinated.

Look around your workplace. Are the people all doing pretty much the same type of work? Do you have similar jobs? If so, then you are grouped by function. You can talk with each other about how to accomplish different tasks. The people in your office or department will have a lot of knowledge about whatever your jobs are about. You are the experts in your organization on this function, such as accounting or marketing. Conversely, you might be grouped with people who have different functions. Do people—or perhaps groups of people—perform very different jobs? Are you working with people who specialize in different areas? Do you all work on the same output, such as a type of service or particular product? This probably is a grouping by product or project, also known as a divisional structure. There are advantages and disadvantages to each method of grouping. There also are other ways to group workers, but these two are the most common.

> Amy and the others in her department designed the packaging for commercial products sold by Terralunarmar. Design work orders came from all the product groups across the company. Amy stayed busy and liked the variety in her work. The CEO of Terralunarmar retired. The new CEO was a fan of divisional structures, and reorganized around product groups. Amy was reassigned to the Xtottier product group. Amy was now the focal point for packaging design just for Xtottier products. She was it. Her coworkers also had been assigned to various product groups. They communicated by tweets, instant messaging, and e-mail but she missed being able to turn to someone nearby and get a question answered.

Amy originally was in a functional grouping. In functional groupings it is easy to talk about functional issues but more difficult to talk about products or projects. If you are in a functional grouping, then those who share your workplace should be knowledgeable about changes in methods, policies, procedures, and laws that affect your function. Amy then was reassigned to a divisional structure. In a divisional grouping specialists in different functions have more difficulty staying informed about their disciplines. Their energies are directed more toward the product or service for which they are the functional representative.

Coordination is the other major factor affecting organizational structure and how people work. Coordination is about who needs to talk with whom, who needs to have information, and who needs to be aware of the activities of others so that everyone is "on the same page." There are different forms of coordination, some involving people above you or below you in the organization, some involving people lateral to you.[5] In vertical coordination things must be coordinated up and down your chain of command. In some cases rules and regulations are in place for all to follow.

Information systems are critical to good coordination both vertically and horizontally. The more coordination is needed, the more the expense and the resources involved. Sometimes a person is a liaison with another organization or part of an organization. That person is in direct contact and insures that coordination occurs when needed. At one time in my career I was a liaison between the General Accounting Office of the United States operating in Europe and the Headquarters for the United States Air Forces in Europe. We talked frequently about GAO auditing activities and I kept my leaders informed.

Another form of coordination is the full-time integrator, a person with much responsibility but no authority. We have an interdisciplinary graduate program at my university. The director of that program is a full-time integrator. He is responsible for staffing courses and coordinating curricular issues but he supervises no one. He works with faculty to staff courses but cannot direct anyone to do so.

Some situations demand very high coordination on an ongoing daily basis. This is where teams can be effective. If what is needed are high levels of interaction and people working together toward a common purpose with the freedom collectively to manage their work, then a self-managed team could be the best option. Teams are most effective in what is called an "organic structure," or in a more mechanistic structure in which decision making is decentralized. This is especially important for virtual teams, who can be located around the world and work together only in cyberspace.

Key: Understand whether your organization's structure is more mechanistic or more organic; this gives you insights into your work and the work of others.

Working in mechanistic organizations is very different from working in organic organizations. Three main dimensions or characteristics determine the degree to which an organization's structure is mechanistic or organic— complexity, formalization, and centralization.[6] These dimensions can be thought of as continuums ranging from high to low.

Complexity largely is determined by specialization. If the organization has high levels of complexity, then you probably are working in a specialized job with a written job description. If the organization has low levels of complexity, then you probably do a wide variety of tasks, perhaps whatever is needed on a given day.

One summer, in my youth, I worked as a common laborer. Each day when I came to work the foreman would assign me things to do. Every day was a little different, with tasks ranging from mixing concrete to cleaning up construction debris. My job was not specialized.

A second dimension is formalization. Does your organization have many policies, procedures, and rules? Most corporations and governments have high levels of formalization. Formalization reduces the need for judgment, reduces variability, and increases consistency in products or services. Why does a McDonald's Big Mac taste the same in every store? It's because McDonald's manuals are very detailed and "cover everything from methods of preparation and quality control to dealing with customers."[7] If the digitized manuals were printed, they would equal hundreds of pages.

Third is centralization. Where are most of the decisions made in the organization? If most are made in the chain of command, then the organization is high in centralization. If centralization is low, then employees are likely empowered and can make many decisions themselves; decisions are made at lower levels. Teams work best in environments where the level of centralization is low; they work worst where the level of centralization is high.

Think about your workplace and these three dimensions—complexity, formalization, and centralization. Larger companies tend toward being high on these three dimensions. This is a mechanistic organization design. Smaller companies tend toward being low on these three dimensions. This is an organic organization design. In larger organizations, workplaces can vary as to whether they are more mechanistic or more organic. The Accounting Department, for example, might be more mechanistic but the Research and Development Department probably is more organic. Whether an organization, or part of an organization, should be more mechanistic or more organic depends on many factors.[8]

Understanding whether your workplace is more mechanistic or more organic helps you decode your workplace. It helps you understand why things are done certain ways. For example, why do certain people make decisions and others do not? Why does your job require adherence to standard procedures, or does not? If there are many rules and procedures, why is that so? These insights about your organizational structure help you understand how well you or others fit with that particular workplace.

Rob left his job as a member of the investment team at one bank to take a similar position at another bank where he was part of a work group. He liked working like this better. Rob was back to feeling like himself again.

The new bank had a benefit Rob especially liked. It would help pay for him to earn his Master of Business Administration degree at a local university. Rob wanted an MBA and started the program. It was in his course on Organization Design that a "light bulb" went on. He realized that banks typically are very mechanistic. Because of a variety of factors, this usually is the best structure for them. The bank where Rob had worked had moved to a team structure throughout. Rob understood now that this structure did not make sense from an organization design perspective. His previous employer had tried to raise productivity but instead actually had reduced it, and many of Rob's friends there were unhappy. The bank had moved toward a more organic structure when a mechanistic structure probably would have been better.

Some people love the structure of a mechanistic organization. They like knowing their specific job, letting their supervisors make the big decisions, and going to the manuals for guidance when needed. Other people prefer the variety of a more organic workplace, being empowered to make important decisions, not having to dot every "i" or cross every "t." There are significant individual differences here. The better the match between your workplace and the type of structure you prefer, the more satisfied you will be.

> **Key: People have informal networks and informal groups about which you might or might not be aware.**

Chapter 2, Systems, introduced the importance of understanding the difference between the formal and informal organization. It emphasized that you should not underestimate the importance of informal groups and networks. The problem is that you might not know about the existence of an informal group—one that can affect your work or your career. You might not know which coworkers know each other nor be aware of the specifics of these relationships.

I returned to my office on a Monday after a week-long consulting trip. A casual acquaintance dropped by my office. After some small talk he remarked, "I heard your team did a great job last week. Sweet." I thought so, too. But how did he know? It turned out that a member of my team attended the same church as my casual acquaintance. They had talked at church on Sunday. I had no knowledge of the relationship. Sometimes you never know.

Next we take a closer look at informal networks and informal groups. Informal networks are composed of informal groups, but not all informal groups are part of informal networks. It is easy to ignore or overlook the importance of informal networks and informal groups.

Think about the relationships you have at work. Some relationships are defined by the organization. These are involuntary. For example, you report to a supervisor. There might be certain people with whom you are required to coordinate for certain actions. These interactions you cannot change. But other relationships you choose. They are voluntary. We can characterize voluntary relationships in different ways based on the purpose of the interactions.

Informal networks are relationships that develop in the workplace and help get the work done. To whom do you go when you need work-related information? Who comes to you for information? Who can you count on to help you sort out a work-related problem? Who do you need on your side when advancing an idea, initiative, or work-related issue? These informal networks naturally arise out of individual strengths, weaknesses, and personalities. They exist when you arrive on your first day of work, but usually no one tells you about them. You have to observe, make mental notes, and learn the informal network by trial and error. Observe how informal communications flow, who listens to whom. Failure to do so could reduce your effectiveness and impact how others might perceive you in the workplace. Here we revisit Laura, whom we met in the first story in Chapter 1, Using Keys to Decode the Workplace.

> Laura had been on the job for six months. She was beginning to understand how work really gets done. She initially had wondered why people kept going to Steve for advice. Now she knew the answer. Steve had a long history with this organization and he knew whom to ask, how to ask, and how to do things. He just was very knowledgeable and was willing to share. She had asked for Steve's help on several occasions. He helped her avoid some pitfalls and gave her some ideas that really made her work easier and better. Her supervisor, Kelly Lorre, turned out to be nice enough but she did not have the depth of knowledge Steve had nor did Kelly have the same number of connections. Laura had gotten to know Molly Sanderly in Marketing and Emilee Bonesal in Accounting over lunches and enjoyed their company. They sometimes got together with a few other office friends on weekends.

Laura's relationship with her supervisor was involuntary. Her relationship with Steve was voluntary. Steve was an important player in the informal network. Laura, Molly, Emilee, and their office friends were an informal group brought together by common interests. They enjoyed each other's company, but their informal group was not part of the informal network in Laura's workplace through which work was done. Had there been a need, Laura could have asked Molly, Emilee, or another friend a work-related question, but this rarely was necessary. Some informal groups in the workplace are mostly social—just people enjoying each other and their shared interests, such as sports, the latest movie, or their families. These groups meet important social needs.

I use these examples to clarify the differences between the formal network, the informal network, and informal social groups. In actuality they are not exclusive. Your boss, for example, could be the boss, a key player in the informal network, and part of your informal social group. In *The Hidden Power of Social Networks,* Cross and Parker described how organizations can perform survey analyses to sort work-related informal groups from more social informal groups.[9] Managers know that work gets done through informal networks but rarely do they try to harness their knowledge of informal networks to improve organizational effectiveness.

Informal groups can grow out of work interactions and further that work, hence they are part of informal networks. Other informal groups, as noted, might be purely social. Informal groups—both in and out of networks—form through interactions. Through interactions we find others who share similarities and have common interests. We just have to interact enough to find what we have in common, or see each other wearing sports jerseys supporting the same team. We might have similar attitudes or values and could develop relations of trust and even respect.

Most workplace groups are formed by proximity or nearness. We are more likely to interact with others who are around us physically than with people who are farther away. Think about where you live. Think about your neighbors. Who do you know best? For most it is the people in the house next door or across the street, or those in the apartment next door. My wife and I have dear friends that we've known for decades and whom we met while I was a graduate student at Purdue. What if we had not purchased the house next door to these wonderful people? Of such choices the fabric of our social lives are made.

For several years I conducted research on organizational smoking policies with Ken Olive, M.D., a Professor of Medicine at East Tennessee State University.[10] We studied one hospital that had an outdoor area where staff members were permitted to smoke. I hypothesized that the staff members who mingled at the designated smoking site would have formed an informal group. This informal group would become more knowledgeable about some hospital activities than people who did not smoke. Why? Because the smokers who gathered in the smoking area worked throughout the hospital. While smoking, people sometimes would discuss work-related issues. People could share their experiences and perspectives drawn from different areas of the hospital. Survey results found this to be the case. One technician commented on how he helped two physicians solve a problem in their area of the hospital by sharing how the issue was handled in his area of the hospital.

Previous chapters of this book discussed norms, roles, and the process of organizational socialization. These apply to both formal and informal groups. Some groups are highly attractive and hence very cohesive; others are less so. In most workplaces there tends to be an "in-group" that gets more visibility and more rewards, and an "out-group" composed of people who have less influence. These in-groups and out-groups can change with turnover in personnel.

In all organizations "grapevines" exist. Grapevines are informal communication channels by which information—and sometimes gossip—is shared among individuals and across organizations. I once worked with an organization with the fastest grapevine I have ever encountered. Information seemed to move through it at the speed of light. One day when I visited this organization, I mentioned something to one of the employees I knew who worked in the first office I passed. By the time I had reached my appointment—ten minutes later and four floors higher in the building— what I had mentioned already was common knowledge. Yes, information sometimes can move that fast through the grapevine.

Organization structures impact how you work and what happens around you. Whether you work in a work group or as a team, the complexity, formalization, and centralization of your organization shapes your day, the nature of your work, and even the people around you. If you understand these structural differences, then you can see aspects of the workplace which often are hidden from others. You might understand why a change in organization structure works or doesn't work. Even better, you might be able to influence organization design decisions. Likewise, if you attend to the informal groups and networks around you, then you will gain insights that others could miss—making you much better at decoding the workplace and more effective in the work at hand.

CHAPTER NINE

Organizational Culture: As Fish Are to Water, People Are to Culture—Unaware

It was Stephen's first visit to a South American country. It had been a productive day doing business for his company. His host, Renardo, suggested they have dinner together.

"Around seven," Renardo suggested. "I'll pick you up at your hotel."

"Sounds good. See you then."

At 7 p.m. Stephen was in the lobby of his hotel waiting for Renardo; 7:30 came and passed; then 8:00.

"Something must have happened," thought Stephen. He checked his phone for messages. There were none. He had Renardo's office phone number but not his mobile number. When 9:00 came and passed Stephen decided to stay cool. This visit could lead to some profitable opportunities. Renardo's company was a major client and Renardo seemed like a solid employee and responsible person. Finally, at 10:00 p.m., Renardo arrived.

"Everything OK?" Stephen asked.

"Sure," replied Renardo. "Just visiting with some friends. I know a great place to eat I think you'll enjoy. Hope you are hungry."

If you have traveled in other countries, you might have noticed differences in how people live and work. People around the world are very similar—we share basic needs for food and shelter and love. The cultures in which we live out our lives, however, are very different. How people view time is one example of a cultural difference. Stephen did not realize he was in a country where "relational" time often is more important than "clock" time. Arriving several hours after a meeting time was acceptable and perfectly normal, especially if one were helping or visiting family or friends. Renardo was not late by his country's cultural norms. As a Brazilian once said to me, "If I arrive on time for a social engagement in my country, it would be considered rude."

Key: Cultural differences and how people behave in different cultures influence the workplace.

Cultural differences are increasingly amplified as business becomes more and more global. As managers work virtually with team members in different countries, cultural differences can cause problems. In a country where people adhere rigorously to a hierarchy of command, for example, making decisions and getting them approved takes longer. As diversity grows within the workplace, the importance of understanding cultural differences also increases.

Few countries share the perspective of the United States business community that "time is money." People who work with Americans might develop this attitude but most will not. As Europe moves toward closer economic integration, norms about work and productivity are coming to the forefront. Closing businesses for several hours in the afternoon is an important part of the culture of Spain, but as more Spanish businesses work with the countries of northern Europe, will the Spanish tradition of siesta survive? Countries vary in when they work and how hard they work. As a Spanish student once said to me, "Time is not money—time is life." In the United States, we rank low among developed nations in the number of vacation days used. Consequently, we rank very high—much higher than Western European nations—for how many hours we spend on the job.[1]

Years ago, when I was a young Air Force officer, I was assigned to an Air Force base in what was then West Germany. When the plane touched down in Frankfurt, I was full of excitement. I was in Europe. My mind raced with centuries of history and peoples and wars and achievements—and here was that land. I was beginning a new job. A new coworker, who was to help with my transition, greeted my wife, our baby, and me at the airport and drove us to our new home an hour away. While my wife and child slept, I just stared out the window. I found it hard to comprehend that I was really in Europe and was going to live here for the next three years. On the Autobahn, cars zipped by at breathtaking speeds, far faster than allowed in the United States. We passed big, slow moving trucks in bright oranges and greens and blues and yellows that no self-respecting U.S. trucker would be seen in. At the rest stop guys just walked onto the grass, unzipped their pants, and let nature take its course while the world watched. As we neared our new home, we passed what appeared to be a very large two-story motel adorned with an enormously large red neon sign, "Sex mit hart." I thought to myself, "Toto, I've a feeling we're not in Kansas anymore."

Countries differ in so many ways, including how close to each other people stand, how they view authority, preferences for rules and structure, the importance of the individual vis-à-vis the group, roles for men and women, and the pace of work. On the larger world stage the clash of cultures is daily news. The realities of globalization bring the forces of technological and economic change into conflict with traditional values and ways of life.[2] Differences in cultures are at the heart of the major stories of our age.

Even within countries we find regional cultural differences. The slower, "chew the fat" way of doing business of the rural South of the United States. The faster, "nothing but the facts" way of doing business in New England. Cities can differ, and within cities we find many subcultures.

If you have not traveled in other countries, you might not have thought much about the rich varieties of human experience, the many ways we live on this planet. But even if you have traveled, you might have only seen surface differences, such as veiled faces, cows wandering the streets, or people queued for a bus. Or you might have experienced different behaviors, such as the gentleman who stands uncomfortably close when speaking to you, the head nodding "no" that means "yes," men who speak only to men. The cultures of countries differ in ways we can see, behaviors we can experience, and deep-seated assumptions we could have difficulty recognizing. The same is true with organizations.

Key: Just as the cultures of countries are very different, so too are the cultures of our organizations.

We might not intuitively understand that organizations differ. Each organization has a culture in which the lives of its members unfold. Like the culture of countries, the cultures of our organizations differ in ways that we can see (if we look), behaviors we can experience (action and words), and deep-seated assumptions we could have difficulty recognizing (if we recognize them at all).

One of the major problems in mergers and acquisitions is a failure to identify differences in organizational culture and how those differences impact the workplace. Cultures often clash in situations such as when an aggressive bank takes over a traditional family bank; a company with a laidback casual culture takes over a company with a suit-and-tie culture; or when a young for-profit hospital merges with a religion-affiliated long-established community hospital. In each case, the dominant organization's culture will impact the other culture, usually negatively. The result can be decreased productivity and morale—and this can last for years. What looked good financially on paper in reality was not necessarily a good idea; but employees must live with the results of these decisions. As you move from one company to another, do not assume the cultures will be the same.

Organizational culture is one of the more difficult organizational concepts to understand and appreciate. We are immersed in it. We live in it. We don't see it. We are like fish swimming in the sea, totally unaware of the water.

So what is organizational culture? Think of it as the beliefs, behaviors, values, and fundamental assumptions that characterize an organization and frame how the organization sees and operates. Some of the norms and roles we have discussed in previous chapters might be embedded in the organization's culture or subcultures. Ed Schein—MIT professor emeritus and organizational scholar—describes three levels of an organization's culture: its visible artifacts, its espoused values and beliefs, and its underlying basic assumptions.[3]

Just as your beliefs, values, and assumptions are reflected to some degree in visible aspects of your life—such as your clothing, housing, car, and charitable giving—an organization's beliefs, values, and assumptions are reflected in visible aspects or artifacts of its workplace. Just as you express attitudes or values that might or might not be consistent with your core beliefs (e.g., "avoid fast food like the plague"), an organization expresses values and beliefs that might or might not be consistent with its core assumptions (e.g., "The customer is always right"). Additionally, just as memories, desires, feelings, and fears in your subconscious work their way into the fabric of your behaviors, an organization has core values and assumptions that have evolved over time—sometimes unstated, often unrecognized—and are woven into the fabric of its organizational life.

Key: The culture of your organization profoundly affects your life in an organization—and in ways you might not recognize.

Culture permeates an organization. It is pervasive, powerful, and enduring. Culture can affect an organization's climate, which is made up of workplace attitudes such as job satisfaction, worker morale, employee commitment, and how much employees participate in decision making. But unlike climate, which is more readily changed, culture is extremely difficult to change once established. It is in the bedrock of the organization and it could take an earthquake to shift the landscape.

The easiest aspects of culture to see are at the artifact level. Artifacts are the visible manifestations of culture. Examples include the physical environment, styles of dress, ways of interacting, and modes of operation. These usually are what a person first notices about an organization. If you walk around the campus of my university, you'll see small classrooms, most outfitted with the latest technology. You'll see students sitting in the quad connected to the Internet through the campus Wi-Fi. In classrooms you'll find a crucifix on the wall and in the center of the campus a statue of St. Joseph and the boy Jesus. From these artifacts you can come to some conclusions about our culture. Some of your conclusions might be right but others might be wrong. Sometimes it is difficult to infer deeper meanings from artifacts only.

If your job takes you in and out of businesses, you know how different businesses can be. Ask the pharmaceutical rep who spends the day going from one physician's office to another. Ask the truck driver delivering goods from store to store. Ask the temporary worker who works in different offices from week to week. If your job does not take you in and out of businesses—especially businesses similar to the one in which you work—you might not notice the cultural aspects of your workplace that outsiders notice.

A young e-commerce company had a good business plan but needed more capital to move to the next level. Jed—a friend of the founder—had a contact, Harold, who could help. Harold examined the financial data and the business plan. A meeting was arranged at the site of the e-business. Jed, who had visited the business several times, toured the business with Harold and the CEO. Harold met the key members of the leadership team and talked with several of the employees, mostly newly minted software engineers. Harold seemed pleased with the answers to his questions.

After the visit, Jed turned to Harold and asked, "So what do you think?"

"Jed, I wish them the best—but not with my money. Did you see that place? I've never seen such a mess. Papers and trash everywhere. I don't know how they can work like that. What they need is a janitorial service but I'm not convinced they would use it."

The mess that Harold saw in the offices reflected the disorderliness of the founder. The founder had built the business working around the clock and living in this office; but as the business grew, nothing changed. The founder never really thought about it—he just didn't care. Consequently, neither did his employees. The papers and trash were just part of the environment, part of the background. But, to an outsider who is accustomed to orderliness in a well-run business, the disorder was very noticeable and it raised questions about what else might not be in order.

Usually the physical environment reflects some aspects of the culture, but it is possible for the physical environment to actually influence the culture or subculture. One of the strangest consulting experiences I ever had was an example of this. A senior official in an organization was concerned about one of his units, a small group of about 12 people. The people in this unit were ineffective in negotiations—even on internal resource issues. They would smile nicely but never showed enthusiasm for any undertaking. Other branches saw them as wimps. The senior official wanted me to talk with them to see if I could come up with any ideas to turn things around.

The offices were located in the basement of a building. The head of the unit greeted me softly, almost a whisper, and then introduced me to his staff, always in a low voice. Each in turn replied in a near whisper. It was obvious you could hear a pin drop in these offices. The acoustics of the basement offices were such that every sound was greatly amplified. People whispered to keep from disturbing each other. I thanked the head of the unit for the introductions and suggested we talk in the cafeteria so we would not disturb the others. We grabbed a cup of coffee and sat down for a chat. "So tell me about your group." I said.

Then, in a soft whisper, he started talking. Every person I interviewed spoke in the same manner. It was an office of low talkers! The employees in this unit had been there for years. They had learned to speak softly and it just carried over outside of their office. No wonder they were seen as unenthusiastic wimps.

A move to new offices fixed the source of the problem, but the behaviors were still ingrained. Over the next six months the soft-speaking subculture changed slowly as employees found their voices. With their stronger voices came greater effectiveness in negotiations.

Schein suggested that sometimes it is difficult to decipher what artifacts mean. In my consulting experience with the low talkers, people heard the soft speech but had not associated it with the physical environment of the office's extreme acoustics. Once it was identified it seemed obvious to all. Moreover, they were somewhat puzzled as to why they had not thought of it themselves. They were like fish swimming in water.

> **Key: Differences between what an organization preaches and what it does could reveal the real core of an organization's culture.**

An organization has some beliefs and values that it openly shares with the world. Other beliefs and values are internal and only discussed among employees. Espoused beliefs and values can be found in mission statements, statements of company values, and slogans. They can be found in stories told to newcomers. These tales are part of organizational lore which point to shared values and ways of doing business. Among the best known of these stories is one involving Tom Watson, Jr., then president of IBM.[4] Here is one version.

> Surrounded by his entourage, Watson entered a company building and was moving through a control point when he was stopped by the security guard.
>
> "Sir, you do not have your identification badge."
>
> Someone in the entourage snorted, "Don't you know who this is?"
>
> To which the guard replied, "Yes, sir. I recognize Mr. Watson. But he is not wearing his badge."
>
> At this point Watson acknowledged the guard's request and sent someone to his office to get his identification badge. He waited. The message was clear. No one is above the rules, not even the CEO.

Stories like this become legend. All companies that have been around for a while have them. The CEO who drops everything to fly to Minnesota to meet with a client to insure a customer's needs are met. The message? "Go the extra mile to insure the customer is satisfied." The CEO whose factory has a fire but who keeps the paychecks going while the factory is put back into operational order. The message? "We are family." The CEO who says "job well done" by flying all employees and their significant others to Hawaii for a vacation at company's expense. The message? "Know that you are appreciated and will be rewarded." Actions can speak louder than words, but significant actions become words that live long beyond the original actions.

At the heart of culture are the core assumptions that pervade organizational life, regardless of whether those in the organization know that. Sometimes the espoused beliefs and assumptions flow accurately and directly from these basic core assumptions. At my academic home, Mount St. Joseph University, caring about the individual student is a deep-seated core value. It is at the heart of who we are—our culture—and is demonstrated in our actions.[5] At "the Mount," faculty, staff, and administrators give extra effort to help students learn and succeed.

My guess is that you might see some gaps between what your organization says and what it does. "Formally, here is what we say. Informally, here is what we do." We say that customer satisfaction is our top priority but actually it is maximizing profits. We say that we value our employees—the backbone of our organization—but to reduce costs we turn first to laying-off employees. We say we have a strong commitment to the community and at the same time we are planning on moving jobs to Mexico.

Sometimes these result from espoused beliefs and values being different from the underlying assumptions. Some assumptions at the heart of culture can be hard to detect when you are part of the culture. Beneath ways of doing things and the decisions made lie assumptions. How does the organization really view employees? Hard working? Lazy? How do we really view our customers? The best? Not too bright? Is responsibility shared? How are people held accountable? Are they? Do we really believe in empowerment? How do we determine strategy? How do we determine opportunity? What do we reward? What do we punish? Do we really care about integrity? There are shared but unspoken answers to such questions at the heart of organizational culture.

If you simply ask these questions of members of an organization, you will elicit the espoused beliefs, not necessarily the real answers. You could develop working hypotheses about what the real answers might be. Over time you might confirm your ideas or find that your answers were not correct after all. Some answers will come with time. Some might come if you advance in the organization. Others will come when someone with the answers trusts you enough to share them with you. Other times insights grow out of specific organizational experiences.

Madison was the company's senior training and development specialist. An excellent instructor, she was always learning, bright, and had a future in the organization. Funds were limited for training so she was surprised to learn that Mark, the CEO, was considering a $30K motivational program for the employees. Madison had read reviews of this motivational program and questioned its value, especially given the other good motivational programs that could be purchased with $30K. She scheduled a meeting with Mark.

"Mark, I heard we're considering the Singing Sponges motivational package. I just wanted to give you my two cents." Madison then laid out her reservations.

Mark thought for a moment and then replied, "OK, Madison. We won't go with the Singing Sponges. You and the other trainers can give me your recommendation on which motivational package to buy. Frankly, I don't

think any of this soft stuff is worth a dime—but I do feel we need to spend
a little money on it every now and then to keep people happy. Let me know
when you have a recommendation."

Mark had shared a basic assumption with Madison: "People programs
aren't really valued much around here." Madison might have suspected
this or figured it out over time but Mark made it clear.

Early in my academic career at the Air Force Institute of Technology
near Dayton, Ohio, I taught management and organizational behavior
courses to engineers pursuing graduate degrees in engineering management. I learned that engineering cultures typically place less value on people skills and more value on technical skills. In other words, the human
factor might be an afterthought. This was a major reason reengineering
efforts of the 1990s usually were not successful.[6] In scrapping the old
process and starting anew, little consideration was given to the importance
of people, the sociotechnical aspects of process, the valuable—and sometimes invaluable—tacit knowledge acquired over time by people who have
been let go.

A few years ago, I attended a conference of an organization which had
been founded by an engineer. The conference was attended mostly by
engineers. The schedule was totally booked with meetings with no breaks
between sessions and no breaks in the day. If you attended a 10:00 a.m.
meeting in one part of the conference center, then you'd have to leave the
session early or you would miss the start of the next. And the sessions
went until very late into the evening. One session started at 10:00 p.m.! In
this case, no thought was given to the people side of things. Engineering
fish swimming in an engineering sea.

> **Key: Culture gives members of an organization a common lens to look through to make sense of events around them.**

Most people in organizations do not realize that they are looking
through a lens. Schein argued that aspects of culture work invisibly and
without our awareness to bring a sense of coherence to organizations. Culture can shape our behaviors without our knowing that our behaviors are
being shaped.

The class I was to teach began at 1:00 p.m. I arrived at the classroom and
opened the door. The class was composed of about 20 students; half of the
students were traditional college age and half of the students were older,

non-traditional age. They were sitting in groups at tables as they awaited the beginning of their class on Organizational Theory and Change. Today, I was not in coat and tie. Today, I wore a blue smock. I stood at the door for a moment and then took off my shoes before entering the classroom. I walked to the blackboard and wrote, "Silence." I then moved to an empty seat in the back of the classroom at a table with several other students. The room was quiet. I opened a brown paper bag and produced a bowl of vegetable soup. Using my hands, I reached into the bowl and scooped some veggies. Lifting the bowl, I loudly slurped the soup. This went on for ten minutes. The room remained silent. When I finished, I put my head down and rested for a few minutes. I then gathered the remnants of my meal, went to the board, erased "Silence," wrote "Discuss," and left the room.

If you had been in that class, what would you have thought?

I cleaned up, changed into a coat and tie, and returned to the classroom. Long before I reached the class, I could hear the sound of students discussing what had just happened. The conversation was loud and animated and involved the whole class. I entered and said, "So, what did you think?"

The class was evenly divided four ways. Some students found the situation "absolutely hilarious" and could not believe a professor would act like that. Others thought it was "a waste of time and money." They were spending hard-earned money to learn something, not for this garbage. Still others were just confused, "I don't have any idea what that was about." And then there were the students who had taken a course or two with me; they told the others, "It's Dr. B., he's trying to teach us something."

The students shared a cultural lens. Our class was embedded in the culture of our educational institution. Although they were not consciously aware of it, the students had expectations about the professor and classroom behavior. The culture of the classroom affected their behaviors. In other words, they had a common lens shaped by the organizational culture by which they could make sense of the classroom and respond accordingly. When I wrote "Silence" on the board, remaining silent was consistent with that lens. As my behavior grew progressively stranger, however, the cultural lens was less helpful. The lens that allowed them to make sense of my behavior, for most of the students, simply did not work. My behavior seemed to be inconsistent with the classroom culture. Instead of a common view of what was happening, they fell back to individual perceptions and their own experiences. My "different" classroom behavior brought the classroom culture into focus for the students. It was a good class that day. I challenged them to think about the organizations of which they are a part and how they might be being influenced by organizational culture without their knowledge.

My deviation from normal classroom behaviors made cultural influences easier to understand. Likewise, significant events in the life of organizations bring cultural influences into focus. After each of the two space shuttle disasters, presidential commissions identified cultural influences at NASA as contributing factors. Sometimes the lens is exposed. We could be so immersed in our organizations, however, that we just don't see the shared lens or the influences of culture. Life goes on and "that's just the way we do things" rules the day. But if we look at artifacts, understand espoused beliefs and values, pay attention to differences between words and actions, and stay alert to significant organizational events, then aspects of organizational culture will be revealed, helping us decode the workplace.

Part V: Influence

CHAPTER TEN

Leaders and Managers: Followers Make Leaders

Justin was excited about joining Johnston Howl's company. He had heard many good things from those who worked for Mr. Howl. Howl's employees worked hard and often put in long hours, but they shared Howl's vision to be number one in customer service in their industry. Mr. Howl was a great CEO. He had big plans for the company. It was a small company now, of just a few hundred people, but it seemed that Mr. Howl knew everyone. There was just something about listening to him talk and speaking with him face to face that made you want to do your best. Justin was very glad for the opportunity to work for such a great leader in an up-and-coming company.

Organizations want leaders, people who can make a difference. Justin perceived Johnston Howl as such a person. Justin was willing to go beyond just doing the job to help Mr. Howl's company succeed. In my opinion this is the real difference between leadership and management.

> **Key: A leader inspires others to go above and beyond the normal requirements of the job.**

There are many books about leadership, what leaders do, and how to be a leader. Business magazines include articles about leadership as frequently as *Cosmopolitan* includes articles about sex. There is an unstated assumption that we know what is meant by leadership, and most of us probably have some idea. We know it when we see it.

Trying to differentiate between leadership and management has a long history in scholarly writings. There is no agreement. John Kotter argued that management is about keeping things functioning and the day-to-day operations, whereas leadership is about producing "useful change."[1] The manager runs the business. The leader provides the vision. You will find this view in many popular writings. The leader does the "vision thing."

Research on leadership dates back nearly a century. At first the questions were, "Are leaders born or made?" and "Can we find the traits of a leader?" We found a few that seem to correlate more than others, including intelligence, a need to be dominant, and self-confidence. But we moved on to other questions, "If they are not born, then how do we make them?" and "Can we identify the behaviors?" After a lot of research, we ended up with two general styles: being people-oriented and being task-oriented. We discovered that the most effective leader behavior depends on the situation. Some argued that you should know your own style and lead where your style fits the situations. Others argued that you should know the situation and adjust your style to that situation.

In my opinion, most "leadership" studies and much of this long research history have studied management, not leadership.[2] In these "leadership" studies, who was studied? Managers. Managers were compared with nonmanagers, or effective managers were compared with ineffective managers. Most research just assumed that managers were leaders. To study a concept, it should be operationally defined. In practical, measureable terms, what are you studying? It is rare for a leadership study to have an operational definition that differentiates leaders from managers. In graduate school I brought this to the attention of one of my professors, that all the "leaders" in these studies were managers. He replied that there is no difference between management and leadership. "Leadership" research and theory are described in textbooks on organizational behavior, usually in a chapter on leadership. But what is it really? It mostly is a chapter about management style.

One of the most popular textbooks on leadership defines it as "the process of influencing an organized group toward accomplishing its goals."[3] How is that different from management? Don't managers influence groups to accomplish goals? In 2001, Zaccaro and Klimoski concluded—as did several scholars before them—that trying to determine a best definition of leadership is "not a useful direction to take."[4] In 2009, Hackman and Wageman summed it up well, saying "There are no generally accepted definitions of what leadership is, no dominant paradigms for studying it, and little agreement about the best strategies for developing and exercising it."[5]

In the past 20 years, most leadership studies conducted have focused on transactional leadership and transformational leadership.[6] Transactional leadership focuses on providing extrinsic rewards to manage day-to-day operations. Transformational leadership is more inspirational, communicating a vision. So, here's my opinion. What the leadership literature calls "transactional leadership" is management. What the leadership literature calls "transformational leadership" is leadership.

Being able to define the differences between leadership and management is not important to understanding what is happening in your workplace. You will know the difference between managing and leading if and when you experience it.

Key: Whether someone is a leader ultimately is a perception, an attribution made by a follower or followers about another person.

Give me a great group of people that is performing well and put me in charge, and I probably will be seen as a good leader. Give me people who perform their jobs poorly and I will not be seen as a leader. Give me a group of people that is not performing well but the situation changes (for example, the group acquires game-changing technologies) and people perform well, and I will be seen as a leader. Ultimately, whether a person is seen as a leader depends on those perceiving that person. Is a person really a leader if some people see that person as being a leader and others don't?

Paula Adesi headed up an operations branch in a company in a service industry. The people who worked for her were first rate—they knew their jobs and took pride in their work. Her branch performed well. It was only natural that upper management saw Paula as a good leader. The branch employees, however, knew better. They saw Paula as self-serving, narcissistic, and two-faced. She presented one side to management and the other side to her branch employees. They knew she was not a leader. Even so, they were not surprised when she was promoted to Assistant VP of Operations.

Narcissistic leaders underscore the perceptual nature of leadership. From your observations you determine whether someone is a leader. If a person is in a leadership position, then if successful they are more likely to be seen as a leader. From this perspective leadership is an attribution.[7] People also can make different attributions about the same person in the same situation. James Meindl concluded that "it is easier to believe in leadership than to prove it."[8]

Not all narcissistic leaders are bad. Hogan, Raskin, and Fazzini found that healthy narcissistic leaders understand their strengths and know when to seek advice from others.[9] Unhealthy narcissists ingratiate themselves with superiors and ignore their direct reports. They fail to listen to other opinions. They think their way always is the best way. They act as if normal rules don't apply to them. They are great at self-promotion.

You have known people that you perceive as leaders. Some you observe from a distance—such as sports stars and people in political offices. Others you observe up close—such as your boss or a friend who leads informally. In my opinion, you experience leadership in the workplace when, in response to another person, you willingly go above and beyond the requirements of your job—taking your effort to another level, and doing so because you want to. The leader inspires you. The best measure of whether someone is a leader is the follower's response.

There are aspects of people that might lead us to think of them as leaders. In the early 1950s Carter and others suggested that there were behaviors or outcomes common to people who are truly great leaders.[10] One is that they have a high level of individual achievement or prominence. They also elevate the performance of those with whom they work. Another aspect is that they are likable; people enjoy being around them. The great NBA player Michael Jordan immediately comes to mind. An incredible offensive and defensive player earning many NBA awards, he elevated the play of those around him, resulting in six NBA championships. Plus his teammates liked him. The Associated Press named him—second only to Babe Ruth—as the greatest athlete of the twentieth century. As a player on the Chicago Bulls, Michael Jordan was a great leader.

Abraham Zaleznik stated that leaders differ from managers just as managers differ from entrepreneurs.[11] They just think and act differently. Coach Bobby Knight probably would agree. When David Cawthon was teaching at Indiana University, Coach Knight was a guest speaker in Cawthon's organizational behavior class. The topic was leadership. The day of the event arrived. Coach Knight took the podium and told the business students, "The first thing you people need to know about leadership is that most of you simply don't have it in you."[12]

House and Baetz argued that it does make sense that some individual differences play a role in leadership.[13] Leadership is a social process; it occurs with respect to others. People with great social skills or who are superb speakers therefore are more likely to be seen as leaders. Who can listen to Dr. Martin Luther King, Jr.'s "I have a dream" speech and not be moved? In the aftermath of the bombing of a church in Birmingham, Alabama, in 1963 that killed four young girls, Dr. King showed another leadership skill. Prominent leaders of the Civil Rights Movement met in the home of the Rev. Ralph Abernathy. When Dr. King arrived, he sat on the sofa and listened attentively to others arguing that they should meet violence with violence. After an hour Dr. King spoke, saying that this was not our way, not our path, not violence—but he had listened. When he finally spoke, he did so persuasively, with great integrity and great eloquence.[14] Violence would not be an option. Dr. King was a great leader.

House and Baetz noted that most leaders probably have a predisposition to be influential. They naturally like to be dominant, to have their ideas command the day, or perhaps they have a need for power. Leadership occurs in relation to accomplishing goals; therefore intelligence, ability, and energy are important.

People have different levels of energy. I have been amazed at times in my life by people who seem to do it all, do it all well, and have time left over. You have probably known a few. You might be that type of person. About 1% to 3% of the population need only four hours of sleep per night. These people seem to do so much they appear to have a permanently installed "on" button. I have read that Bono, the lead singer of U2, is one of these people. This is not surprising given that he seems to be everywhere doing everything—helping the people of Africa, talking to world leaders, and still living his music. Historical accounts suggest that Benjamin Franklin, Thomas Jefferson, and Leonardo da Vinci were among those who required little sleep.[15]

It seems reasonable that some individual differences enable leaders to succeed, even in difficult situations. Sometimes it can be because of difficult situations. We say Winston Churchill was a great leader during World War II. Would we have been inclined to say so prior to WWII? And was Michael Jordan still seen as a leader when he played minor league baseball, played for the NBA Wizards, or was owner of the Charlotte Hornets? David Cawthon wrote, "There is considerable evidence that the ultimate effectiveness of leaders is significantly influenced by environmental factors. . . . One need not be a philosopher to conclude that there may be a linkage between leadership and the situations in which leaders find themselves."[16]

Leadership can be a nebulous concept. We know people who we think are leaders. We know when we work with someone who inspires us to do more than just meet the basic requirements of the job. I have said that most leadership research actually is research about management styles. That research is important and has much to offer us in understanding managers and decoding the workplace.

Key: Managers are people-oriented, task-oriented, or both, and the best style usually depends on the situation.

People have different beliefs and attitudes about other people. These beliefs and attitudes can affect behavior. Do you think people are lazy? That people will avoid work if possible? That they will try to do as little as possible for the greatest pay? Or do you think people are responsible, that they seek opportunity? That, given the chance, they will be innovative and creative? Or does it depend? If so, then upon what?

> As the furniture store grew, it needed a full-time supervisor for furniture deliveries, so Emerico was hired. After a sale, Emerico would work with the customer to schedule the delivery. He saw his job as a continuation in the value chain for the customer. Delivery must be prompt and professional. Installation, if required, must be done correctly the first time.
>
> Emerico soon learned that complaints about deliveries were common. The delivery crews were not taking time to install items correctly. Mattresses were damaged because employees dragged them on the ground as they raced to complete deliveries. Why were employees in such a hurry? If they finished early, then they could take off the rest of the day.
>
> Emerico knew he had a problem. People were naturally lazy. He couldn't be out supervising all deliveries. He knew what he had to do. Emerico started firing people and replacing them with people he thought might do the job the way it was supposed to be done in return for the wages offered.

Emerico was what Douglas McGregor would call a "Theory-X" manager.[17] He managed using the "carrot-and-the-stick." His assumptions about people were that they were lazy and disliked work. This was typical of most managers at the beginning of the industrial age. In the 1920s, supervisors usually did not give mill workers rest breaks during the day. Why? Because supervisors thought employees were lazy and they should be working.

Also in the 1920s and 1930s, Elton Mayo conducted research at Western Electric's Hawthorne Works, in Cicero, Illinois. The results of his studies challenged traditional views of the worker. Through experiments in the factories and interviews with workers, a different picture emerged. People had needs. They sought intrinsic rewards, such as a satisfying job and meaningful work. The prevalent view that people only were motivated by money was wrong. The Human Relations school of management grew out of this awareness. Managers needed training in human relations because they did not understand their employees or how to best motivate them.

> Julie was meeting with the Director of Human Resources at the headquarters of the global company for which she worked.

"Julie, we were wondering if you'd be interested in working at one of our sites in China. You are a good employee. Your supervisor has told us you have an interest in East Asia. Is that so?"

"Actually, I am very interested in East Asia. It is a part of the world we need to understand. I know it is an enormous future market for us. And I do have a personal interest. I studied Japanese and Chinese Art History in college and was fascinated. I would love the opportunity to learn more firsthand."

"It sounds like you are interested. Let me tell you more about the position and if you would want it, it's yours."

Julie's company appears to have embraced a "Theory-Y" management philosophy integrating organizational and individual needs.[18] The company needed someone for a position in China and Julie was a good fit. The Theory-Y manager understands that if an employee is committed to organizational goals, and these goals meet personal needs, then the employee will accept responsibilities and will be more likely to do well in that position.

So what have been your experiences? You might have seen managers of both types. Some managers think that people have to be driven to produce. Others think that employees just need a fair deal and they will do fine. Are people naturally lazy? Given the range of human behavior, yes, there are probably some who are. Do people want responsibility and opportunities? Again, most probably do. In decoding the workplace, you should be able to get an idea of a manager's assumptions about people from the manager's actions.

More than 50 years ago, studies conducted by the Ohio State University concluded that there were mainly two management styles.[19] Some managers are people-oriented. They show concern for employees, try to support their employees as best they can, and emphasize good working relations among employees. This style comes more easily to managers who have people skills, that is to say relational skills. Other managers are task-oriented. They clarify tasks, establish schedules, emphasize standards, and instruct on how things are to be done. This style comes more easily to managers who have strong organizational skills and who can keep employees doing the job at hand. Many managers use both people-oriented and task-oriented management styles.

Researchers at Ohio State thought that the best managers would be those who did use both styles. Studies found this was not always the case. Sometimes the best manager was someone who was very task-oriented. At other times, it was someone who was very people-oriented. The researchers realized that the best management style depended on the situation.

At the University of Washington, Fred Fiedler's research suggested that managers should know whether they are task-oriented or people-oriented.[20] If the workplace called for someone with people skills, then that was the environment in which the people-oriented manager would be most effective. If the situation was very structured, was an environment in which every "i" must be dotted and every "t" crossed, where strong attention to detail helps, then a task-oriented manager would be most effective. If the situation needed to be organized, needed to be structured, then again the task-oriented manager should excel. If possible, try to structure the situation to fit your style.

Leadership researchers Evans and House took a different approach.[21] They agreed with Fiedler that some management styles are better than others in certain situations. But they suggested altering your management style to fit the situation. If the employees have frequent interaction with each other, customers, or suppliers, perhaps they do not need a people-oriented manager. If a task needs structure, then the task-oriented manager can help provide it. There's also another implication here. If the employees have significant interpersonal interaction and their work is heavily structured, then the manager does not have to be as engaged. The research literature has not resolved these different conclusions about how to apply management styles.

Based on my interpretation of the literature and my consulting, here is how I see it. Some managers are task-oriented. It is who they are. They should not try to change.

I had a boss once who was told by his boss to get out from behind his desk and walk around. His boss believed strongly in managing by walking around. My boss asked me what I thought. Should he give it a try?

I said, "Sir, if you do that, start just walking around, you are going to scare people. They're going to wonder what they are doing wrong. They'll think, 'Why is he here?' No, sir, you'd just cause more problems and you don't need more problems."

He smiled, almost a smile of relief, and said, "Thank you."

The good leaders want honesty. My boss was a task-oriented manager to the "nth degree." He drove his organization but people respected him. He had risen to a high leadership position probably because of his analytical and decision-making acumen, but he did not have strong people skills.

Conversely, some people are "people" people. They enjoy interacting with others, helping them with their problems, guiding teams or groups. Asked to start a project from scratch, a small voice deep inside would say "Run!" Given an environment that is highly structured, they might be alright but probably would not be as effective as they would be when the tasks have more give-and-take.

Some people are both task-oriented and people-oriented. Imagine a continuum. On one end are people who are people-oriented, on the other end are the people who are task-oriented. These managers only can be effective with one style. The managers toward one end of the continuum should try to stick with situations that match their style. In the middle are people equally comfortable and effective with both styles. They should use the style that best fits the situation. Then there are the rest of us who can use both styles to some degree but tend to be better at one than the other.

In the workplace, a manager who is task-oriented in a situation that does not require it could seem like a fish out of water. Likewise, a people-oriented manager in situations of very high or very low to no structure easily could struggle. Observing your manager and other managers can provide some working hypotheses about how well their styles match the workplace.

> **Key: An effective relationship with your boss increases the likelihood of success in your job.**

So what does having an effective relationship with your boss mean? Addressing the Department of Business Administration at the London School of Economics in 1933, Mary Follett talked about something of "the utmost importance, but which has been far too little considered, and that is the part of the followers in the leadership situation."[22] Followers have an active role to play, to help their boss, and to offer suggestions. It is not sufficient just to do what one is told. John Gabarro and John Kotter are more direct. They say that you should manage your boss.[23] Manage or not, your success in the workplace will depend to a large degree on your ability to have a good working relationship with your immediate supervisor.

So how is your relationship with your boss? Great? Good? Poor? You and your boss are mutually dependent on each other. Your boss occupies a position higher in the hierarchy of your organization. Your boss can argue on your behalf with superiors, try to secure for you needed resources, and share information that might assist in your work. Conversely, the boss needs you to perform your job well, to provide ideas for improvement, to be honest in your statements and actions. If you do well, your boss has a better chance of doing well. Part of the boss's success depends on you.

> Keith and Leah worked for Luis Mequela, serving local clients. One day Keith spoke to Leah as she returned from yet another client visit.
> "Leah, you sure spend a lot of time visiting your clients. I don't get it. You could just as easily call them or e-mail them to get the info you need."

"Just trying to do what Mr. Mequela asked us to do. Remember that meeting last month when he suggested we get to know our clients better? For me the best way to do that is to go to the clients and listen to them. I know it takes more time but I am hoping it will pay off."

Just then Mr. Mequela dropped by their office.

"Leah, my boss just got a call from Graenbi Services. They are increasing their orders. They specifically mentioned how impressed they were that a vendor actually took the time to visit and see what they really needed. Anyway, thanks. Nice work."

Leah made her boss, Mr. Mequela, look good with his boss, and Mr. Mequela appreciated it. The odds are this will be to Leah's advantage at some point, especially if she continues to get good results from her client visits. You have a relationship with your boss by function of the formal organization. To a great degree the effectiveness of that relationship, regardless of whether you like your boss, is up to you.

Try to understand your boss. Gabarro and Kotter put it this way: "At a minimum, you need to appreciate your boss's goals and pressures, his or her strengths and weaknesses. What are your boss's organizational and personal objectives, and what are his or her pressures, especially those from his or her own boss and others at the same level?"[24] Know your boss's blind spots, preferred working style, preferred communication patterns, and how your boss deals with conflict.

In a classic *Harvard Business Review* article in 1977, Wickham Skinner and W. Earl Sasser listed attributes of management style.[25] Their list suggests questions that make a good starting point for thinking about your boss.

- Does your boss tend to be more intuitive or analytical?
- Does your boss make decisions unilaterally or consult with others?
- Does your boss make fast decisions or take time?
- Is your boss flexible in opinion or doggedly single-minded?
- Does your boss like or dislike delegating?
- Is your boss usually available or just occasionally?
- Does your boss have a lot of rules to follow or just a few?
- Is your boss's pace relaxed or hectic?
- Is your boss supportive or demanding, even challenging?

To this list I would add, "Is your boss task-oriented, people-oriented, or both?" I also would add, "Is your boss a listener or reader?" Peter Drucker wrote, "Very few people even know that there are readers and there are listeners, and that very few people are both. Even fewer know which of the two they themselves are."[26] Some bosses prefer to talk about issues, listen to opinions, and as needed have subordinates follow-up with something in writing. Other bosses are the opposite. They prefer to get an e-mail, memo, or report—something in writing. They like to read it and think things over before engaging in conversation on the issue. Do you know whether your boss is a reader or listener?

If you can answer most of these questions, then you probably understand your boss fairly well. If you cannot, then you have some work to do. Without such information you are "flying blind when dealing with the boss, and unnecessary conflicts, misunderstandings, and problems are inevitable."[27] It is your job as a subordinate to adjust to your boss's style. It is not the other way around. Know your boss and adapt.

If you know your boss's goals, you will have a better idea where you can help, what you might do. You could be able to offer suggestions—they might or might not be used, but good bosses will appreciate the effort. It can often be difficult for those in leadership positions to get honest feedback.

Akeem worked in a small firm of construction engineers. They consulted and worked on a wide variety of projects. Akeem specialized in electrical engineering. One day he was in the office of the CEO, Brooke Jasonete, when the conversation was interrupted by a phone call. It was a business matter, an engineering issue that had to be addressed so Brooke took the call. Finishing the conversation, she said, "I understand. I'll have one of the boys give you a call," and with that she hung up. Akeem cringed a little. He had heard Brooke call the engineers "boys" on several occasions. He did not like it. Among the "boys," it was something that they joked about. Most did not think anything of it but it bothered Akeem and several others.

"Brooke, a small matter. Several times I've heard you refer to the engineers as 'the boys'. We're all men and highly qualified engineers. I'm not sure calling us boys creates the best impression."

Brooke thought for a moment, and then said, "Akeem, you are absolutely right. I have never thought about that before. I grew up with three brothers and they are still 'the boys' to me. But your point is valid. I appreciate the feedback." And she never called the engineers "boys" again.

Leaders need followers who are not afraid to speak out and who will tell the truth. The very best leader-follower relationships are relationships of trust. Mary Follett suggested that, in the leadership situation, both the leader and the followers are following an "invisible leader—the common purpose."[28] Understanding your boss and your relationship with your boss will make both of you more effective in pursuing the common purpose.

CHAPTER ELEVEN

Power and Influence: Do Favors, Be an Expert, and Understand Perceptions

Ryan was sitting at his desk talking with Steve when Sarah entered his office.

"Can either of you guys help me? I need to move a few boxes to the storage room and they are kinda heavy for one person."
"Sorry, Sarah," Ryan replied. "I'm up to my you-know-what in alligators."
"I'll give you a hand," Steve said. And he did.

Regardless of whether Steve knew it, by doing a favor for Sarah he increased his personal power, his ability to influence. Sarah is now more likely to reciprocate with a favor for Steve than for Ryan, all things being equal.

For many people, if not most, "power" is a negative word. Just hearing the word makes some people cringe. We think of manipulative people, abusive managers, powerful but inconsiderate folk who will step on anyone to get their way or move toward the top. The history of our species is replete with stories of power gained, wielded, and lost. Like it or not, you must understand the dynamics of power to decode the workplace—and to be more effective.

Power simply is the capacity to influence. People, groups, and organizations try to influence you throughout your day, every day. Whenever someone or something tries to influence your behavior, your attitudes, your thoughts, or your decisions, power is involved. Anytime you try to influence the behaviors, attitudes, thoughts, or decisions of others, power is involved. Something as simple as asking for help in moving some boxes involves power. You cannot avoid power and its use. You cannot avoid attempts to influence you. You can, however, understand the dynamics of power, thus having more insight into activities around you in the workplace You can develop your own ability to influence, increasing your effectiveness. This chapter and the next are about power.

> **Key: Power is essential to get things done with or through others.**

We work with others. We work in relation to others. We are assigned duties and tasks that require interacting with others, getting information from others, and getting reports, products, help, and many other things from other people. In all organizational activities people must influence other people to accomplish organizational and personal goals.

Every time you try to get someone or some group to do something, you are using power, regardless of whether you recognize it. Psychologists John French, Jr., and Bertram Raven described five bases of power.[1] Sometimes people do what you ask because you are the boss (power based on legitimate authority). Even if you are not the boss, you could have the ability to affect outcomes others desire (reward.power) or the ability to make life less pleasant (coercive power). Some people will follow you because they see you as "knowing your stuff" (expert power). Others might see you as just a nice person who is fun to be around, perhaps even charismatic (referent power). The stronger your base, the greater your power.

> Melissa and Heather were co-workers. They were not great friends but they got along pretty well. Both were working late one night. Melissa was just finishing up a report for their boss and wanted to be sure everything was right.
>
> "Heather, would you mind looking over these numbers. I need a fresh pair of eyes. I want to be sure that these numbers are correct."
> "No problem," Heather said, "I'll get to it in a few minutes." Heather reviewed the numbers, which were fine.
> "Thanks, Heather. Much appreciated."

Melissa needed a favor. Heather had a choice. Melissa had no authority to require Heather to help; she wasn't Heather's boss. Nothing suggests that Heather saw Melissa as an expert or as a person with whom she particularly enjoyed working. But in the day-to-day life of the office, a good working relationship with Melissa was in Heather's best interest. Someday she might need a favor. If she said no, then Melissa might become uncomfortable to work around for a while. Heather had reward and coercive bases of power and so did Melissa. Heather had the power to help Melissa or to make Melissa's life more difficult by not helping her. Neither Heather nor Melissa would likely see this exchange in terms of social influence or power, but it is both at the most basic level. The simplest office exchanges can involve the dynamics of power.

Understanding power helps you understand what is really happening around you in the workplace. People can have significant power and not be in positions of authority. People can be in positions of authority and not have a clue how to effectively use the power of their positions. We vary widely in our capacity to influence, our knowledge of power dynamics, and our use of power. Some people naturally understand the dynamics of power but, in my opinion, most do not.

To decode the effects of the dynamics of power in the workplace requires understanding the ways that power is developed and used. I have benefited significantly professionally and personally from insights about power by two giants of management thought, John Kotter and Rosabeth Moss Kanter, both at the Harvard Business School. In this chapter and the next, I share and discuss those insights. These chapters provide a foundation in understanding workplace power dynamics. They also are a primer on how to build your power. You probably already are doing some of the activities that are discussed, but you might not have thought about how these activities are related to developing your personal power.

Regardless of your position, you can be more effective if you understand how what you do and say helps build your power. Power is not a dirty word. Rather, power can be a positive word, even a word of hope. Do you want to make a difference in the workplace? In your community? For your family? For those you love? If so, then you need to understand power—how to develop it and how to use it appropriately.

Key: If you do a favor for someone, they are more likely to do a favor for you.

One of the most important ways to build personal power is to be willing to do favors for others. Doing favors for others creates a sense of obligation.[2] When someone does us a favor, we usually feel obligated to reciprocate. "You scratch my back; and I'll scratch yours." This might sound manipulative and it can be.

I knew someone who was notorious for giving a friend or acquaintance an unexpected gift and then a few weeks later, asking a favor. "Oh, by the way, I have some great tickets to the Knicks Saturday night that I can't use. Would you like to have them? On me." Then after a few weeks, "Say, Zach, could you give me a hand? Probably take an hour or so." Everyone knew the gifts preceded requests for favors, but nobody minded. The gifts were great and the favors relatively small. All parties in the exchange were satisfied.

It should not take you long to identify these people. You then can decide whether you want to go along. This is a deliberate tactic used by some to influence others—and it can be manipulative. But doing favors and building power by doing favors does not have to be manipulative.

In the course of a day, we encounter many people—in the workplace; in our communities. Occasionally, we have opportunities to help someone, provide assistance, or answer a question. Sometimes people ask for help. Other times they might not express the need until asked, "Can I help you?" A coworker who needs help moving a desk. A new employee who needs directions to someone's office. Someone too busy to catch lunch who would love it if you picked up a burrito for them when you go to Chipotle. Most of these opportunities take just a brief moment in our day—and yet we might pass them by.

My recommendation is simply to foster a positive attitude toward helping others and doing favors as they arise. Think of it as just being a nice person. "Hold on," you say, "People will take advantage of you." Yes, of course there are people who will take advantage of you. Write them off. Don't do them any favors—just say "no." The advantages here outweigh the disadvantages. "Being nice" does not mean you can't be smart, strong, or tough. Regardless of your intention in doing someone a favor (toward a favor in return or just to be helpful), the result is the same. Doing favors builds a sense of obligation so that a request from you has a greater likelihood of success. In other words, it increases your influence with that person. When doing a favor, you might have no idea when—or if—the favor might be returned.

Scott worked in the regional office of a major agribusiness. An agronomist, he studied the effects of various chemicals on crop production. One day he got an e-mail from a low-ranking official at corporate headquarters, Holly Meade. The following week Meade was flying out to Scott's location. Although she was there on other business, she wanted to learn more about the company's chemical suppliers, all located near Scott. Scott's schedule for that week was brutal but he replied that he'd meet with Holly and see what he could do.

After thinking about this for a while, Scott realized that this was an opportunity to educate someone at headquarters about their local suppliers. It might not directly affect his work but it might be good for Meade, and perhaps for the company. It also really would not take much of his time. With a few phone calls, Scott arranged a tour of local suppliers.

When Holly arrived, Scott gave her an overview of local suppliers and then had Brittany, one of his direct reports, accompany Meade on the tour. Later Scott met Holly and Brittany for dinner and talked with them about their day. Scott's efforts to assist Meade had not been very time consuming, but the benefits to Meade were great. Meade was very appreciative. That was the last time Scott met or talked with Meade for two years.

Two years later, Scott was promoted to chief agronomist and relocated to corporate headquarters. Soon after he arrived, he had an issue that he needed to discuss with the CEO. Scott was told that it took weeks to get on the CEO's schedule. To see if he could shorten the time, Scott went to the CEO's office. Who had an office right next to the CEO's? Holly Meade. She now was the executive assistant to the CEO. Meade immediately recognized Scott and thanked him again for that day two years ago and told him how immensely helpful it had been. Scott was put on the CEO's schedule later that day.

You never know when a favor will be returned. During his time at corporate headquarters Scott had no problem getting issues and ideas to the CEO.

Key: People seen as experts have more influence, usually proportional to the perceived value of their expertise.

Being known for your expertise builds personal power.[3] If you are recognized as having expert knowledge, skills, or abilities, then that expertise can open doors and provide opportunities. Anyone and everyone can be an expert in different ways and to different degrees. Early in my career an Air Force colonel told me, "Know your job better than anybody else —and you'll be an expert." I wrote those words on a note card and kept it under the plexiglass on top of my desk. In the workplace being an expert really can be as simple as knowing your job better than anybody else does.

Kayla processed medical claims. But she did more than just process the claims. She studied the forms, the procedures, the guidelines, and the software. She was naturally curious and just wanted to understand her job. As a result, Kayla's understanding of her job was superior to that of other processors. Coworkers turned to her when there were questions. Her supervisor noticed that Kayla consistently processed claims quickly and with few errors—and that she always could support her decisions knowledgeably. When a change in procedure was proposed from higher ups, Kayla's supervisor always got her opinion. When Kayla's supervisor changed jobs, Kayla was offered the supervisor position.

Think about the people you know and their areas of expertise. We all have our talents, although sometimes we have yet to discover them! Who do you turn to when you have a question in the workplace? A question about a computer? Your car? A new movie? People who are sought out for their opinions, people who are recognized for their expertise have influence. Some bricklayers are better than others. Some carpenters are better than others. Some accountants are better than others, as are some salespeople and some managers, and so on. For the best—for those seen as being experts—there come opportunities others do not have.

My dad was a bulldozer operator. He was an expert. He could make that dozer dance and lay a grade right on the money. I can remember a representative of a major construction company in our modest home offering my dad great pay and other benefits to take a position and relocate, which he declined. I can remember my dad leaving in the morning at 6 a.m. and going to the airport where a company plane awaited. He would be flown to a job site many miles away, where he'd work all day and then be flown home to sleep in his own bed. Then he would do it all again the next day. He was that good.

Sometimes others perceive us as having expertise that we might not have recognized ourselves. During a hot time in the Cold War, key Air Force commanders and senior officers in Europe met to resolve an immediate crisis. The conference room was full of generals and colonels who discussed the situation, what happened, how it happened, and the options to deal with the situation. At some point in the deliberations my commander invited me, a junior officer, into the room.

"Ballard, for your info, you're here because I know you can write," the commander stated.

Being in that room was an eye-opening experience. The senior officials debated until early evening, hammering out their proposed recommendations for the Air Force Chief of Staff at the Pentagon. Then they adjourned. At this point my commander gave me the rough draft of the memorandum containing the recommendations.

"Our office is responsible for getting this in final form for the Air Staff. Ballard, I know this thing is a mess. You heard what we are trying to do. Clean this up, rewrite as you need to, and have this on my desk by 6 a.m."

And I did. The only reason I was in that room was that my commander perceived I could write an organized, to-the-point, well-supported memorandum.

That experience also made other jobs a tad easier. "Haven't I seen you somewhere. Oh, yeah, that meeting. So what can I do for you today?" Being seen as having some expertise builds credibility. Kanter has suggested that credibility equals competence plus power.[4] People who are credible "know their stuff" and also know how to get results.

Part of knowing your stuff is staying current on the latest information which might affect your work. People vary in the degree to which they seek information. People who have information or know how to find information build power. How well do you stay up to date on trends in your business? Are you a member of professional associations? Do you read trade publications? We cannot stay on top of everything—it's impossible. But there are sources of information that—even if only skimmed regularly—could provide an advantage in the workplace, make us more knowledgeable, and help us to know our jobs better than anybody else does.

> **Key: The more a person sees things they have in common with another person, the more that person is likely to help the other.**

We are more likely to help or respond to a request from someone with whom we share interests and experiences.[5] If you like people and find them interesting, the fostering or finding similarities probably comes naturally to you. If you are not terribly interested in others, then finding commonalities might be more difficult. You could find that you enjoy others who obviously share your interests, but you might easily dismiss others who on the surface do not appear to share your interests. With a little effort you might find commonalities with most people.

We need other people. Few of us could retreat into the mountains and live as a hermit. In our deepest core we want to be accepted by others, liked by others. Abraham Maslow suggested that we all have a need to love and be loved. At perhaps an unconscious level, we see interactions with others—especially revealing interactions—as having risks. We want to be accepted but we do not want to risk rejection. We each find different ways to play out this scenario in our lives. Some people take the risks, others build facades. Some people simply avoid interactions as much as possible.

In the workplace we cannot avoid interactions. The social chitchat—the social interactions that take place before getting down to business—these lubricate our organizations, making immediate and other tasks easier. Why is it that the "no-nonsense" person, the person who does not engage in social chitchat, rarely builds strong peer or subordinate relationships? Because it is in these brief social interactions that we find and foster similarities with coworkers.

As we interact with others in different situations, we use behavioral, social, and verbal scripts that we have learned along the way. Think about what we do when meeting a person for the first time. We tend to use safe, low-risk scripts, "How about this weather?" or "Looks like it might rain today." Our conversation and subsequent conversations are like peeling an onion; we gradually expand the range of topics and, in so doing, we start to find similarities. "Did you see the Red Sox game last night?" "Going skiing this weekend?" "I saw a great movie." As people find these similarities, they become more comfortable with each other and a relationship develops. We even might interact more with a person with whom we are comfortable versus taking the time to get to know a new person in the workplace with whom we might have far more in common. If you skip these initial scripts and jump directly into more substantive issues—such as politics—when you do not yet know the other person's views, you take a great risk.

> Dustin and Corey worked on the same floor in the same company. Dustin had been in his position only a few months and he and Corey did not inter-act except on business. Dustin sometimes had to coordinate contracts with Corey. Corey had to look over the contracts and be sure everything was consistent with budgetary guidance. When Dustin dropped off contracts for review, Corey always was too busy to do more than acknowledge the request, "I'll get to it." Eventually he did—but actions that Dustin's prede-cessor had completed in a week were taking Corey two weeks or more.
>
> Realizing that Corey was fairly new to his job, Dustin explained the need for a faster review, but it did not make any difference. Corey's reviews were starting to become a bottleneck and a problem for Dustin. He decided that, if things did not improve very soon, he would have to take the matter to Corey's boss. Dustin didn't like causing trouble for people—especially a recent hire—but he had given Corey just about all the slack available.
>
> But luck intervened. It was a Saturday afternoon. Dustin volunteered as an assistant scoutmaster in a local Boy Scout troop. This was the weekend of the big camporee when all the local Boy Scout troops camped together

and competed in tent raising, rope tying, fire starting, and other scouting activities. As Dustin watched members of his scout troop struggling to start a fire without matches, he heard a familiar voice.

"Dustin, good to see you. I didn't know you were in scouting."

There beside him stood Corey, also in an assistant scoutmaster uniform. Corey and Dustin exchanged the scouting handshake and then shared tales and stories of their scouting experiences and adventures. They had very much in common.

The next week Dustin took Corey a contract for review.

"Dustin, great to see you. I'll review this later today and have it for you first thing tomorrow."

In this scenario, the only difference from one week to the next was Corey had discovered his similarities with Dustin. Dustin never again had a problem with Corey. In fact, they became good friends and together were able to work issues to the benefit of the company and their careers. In this case, there was no deliberate effort on Dustin's part to foster similarities but similarities were discovered. Once discovered, Dustin's requests were seen in a different light and received a higher likelihood of compliance. In this case, much higher.

Be open to finding commonalities with others. Sometimes this means just being more aware. I am cursed with being naturally curious about so many things, including others. When I walk into someone else's office, I just naturally scan the room, the pictures, the knick-knacks, and other personal items. Usually something will catch my eye—a mug that says "Purdue," a painting of the Cape Hatteras lighthouse, a photograph of a daughter playing soccer. For me, each of these items is a conversation starter; they suggest potential commonalities and aid in engaging in brief chitchat. I do not engage deliberately to foster similarities; I just like getting to know people. Regardless, the effect is the same. Whether we do so intentionally or not, finding similarities inherently increases our influence with others and vice versa.

> **Key: People who control resources that others depend on (or who are perceived to control such resources) have greater power.**

John Kotter writes about how effective managers make other people feel dependent on them.[6] People perceive, accurately or inaccurately, that the manager can help or hinder, reward or punish. The more strongly people perceive the manager to be instrumental to some end, the more power the manager has.

The same holds true regardless of whether you are a manager. If people perceive you as being able to help them or hinder them, make their lives easier or more difficult, then you will have more influence with those people. Every job depends on other people. We all have others who depend on us in one way or another—for information, for action, for help—and those upon whom we must depend. Why are secretaries or administrative assistants potentially so powerful? It's because much of the coordination of the business of the workplace depends on them. To decode the workplace, we need to understand who depends on whom.

Sometimes we forget or fail to recognize the inherent interdependencies of the workplace. We make decisions without considering all of the people who will be affected. We make decisions without getting information from people whose input would improve the quality of those decisions. We make decisions without being aware that a successful outcome for our decision depends upon someone else.

In the workplace, what contributes to others' perceptions of being dependent on you? What decisions do you make? What resources do you control? What information can you provide? How does your work affect the work of others? You might have more power than you realize. Regardless, you might wish to examine your job. Are there ways to make your work more important to more people? Can you acquire more resources? Do you have information that more people could use in addition to those who receive it now?

"Quality guru" Philip Crosby told a story, from early in his career, of how he got the attention of senior management in the company where he worked as a quality engineer.[7] No one paid much attention to quality. No quality metrics were reported at meetings of senior management. Crosby was invited to one of those meetings to say a few words about quality. After a three-hour meeting when everyone was ready to leave, Crosby was given the last five minutes to speak. He took only one minute. He simply reported the cost associated with the company's failure to ensure product quality. Crosby stated it in terms of a percentage of the company's earnings—and it was a significant percentage—and then sat down. Quality metrics became part of the metrics reported to and monitored by the senior management team. By stating the impact of his work in terms of costs and profit, Crosby and his staff became more important to the company.

Sometimes a perception is created in which a person is seen as potentially instrumental to others but in reality is not. This could be inadvertent or deliberate. When I was responsible for personnel testing throughout the United States Air Force, I worked for the organization that handled assignments and relocations for military members of the Air Force. I had nothing to do with that aspect of the organization. Even so, people sometimes thought I might be able to help them get a position at a different Air Force base. When I visited Air Force bases, I often was treated better than I would have expected. I never encouraged anyone to treat me differently or misled anyone about my job; the perception naturally occurred.

Conversely, some people deliberately create impressions of resources or connections that are not what they seem. Some people give the impression of being able to influence events when they cannot, of having or being able to get information when they cannot, of having access to needed resources when they don't. Some people imply such concepts without stating something outright—thus planting the perception but maintaining the ability to deny it. Others display pictures of themselves with powerful people just to suggest to others that they have powerful connections, which might or might not be the case. I do not recommend intentionally planting misleading perceptions or implying more than you might be able to deliver. To decode power in the workplace, however, it is important to understand that there are those who do work to create such perceptions.

More about Power and Influence: Choose Activities Carefully and Build 360-Degree Relationships

The project was significant but routine. Elgin had a year to complete the project, a team of 24, and a budget of $1.2 million. There was nothing unusual about what was required to get the job done. Many others at the company had led similar projects. The project management steps were laid out clearly in the company's operations manual. Even so, Elgin pondered how to proceed, this being his first time as project chief. He decided to use a Program Evaluation and Review Technique (PERT) to find the critical steps. His PERT analysis suggested that if he took a different approach to one of the steps in managing the project—an approach different than that specified in the manual—then Elgin might be able to complete the project in six months with a team of 12 and for only $600,000. He checked and rechecked his work. All he needed was the company's approval to try a different approach. There was risk involved but the payoffs could be significant.

Elgin made his case first to his boss and then to officials higher up in the company. Although the bosses were hesitant, they agreed to let Elgin give it a try. Elgin creatively modified the way the critical step was accomplished and finished the project in five months with a team of 12 and for $500,000. Elgin was asked to rewrite the steps in the operations manual, and his approach became the standard operating procedure for these projects in the company.

Elgin went beyond the normal requirements of his job. He took a risk. In some companies taking a risk and failing is the "kiss of death." In other companies it is considered part of learning. Regardless, Elgin took a chance. His effort—for good or ill—was extraordinary; that is, he did far more than just what was expected. It paid off. He demonstrated a different way to handle projects that were an important part of the bread-and-butter operations of the business. This was both relevant to the company and visible to management. Elgin subsequently was fast-tracked for bigger and better opportunities in the company.

In *Men and Women of the Corporation*, Rosabeth Moss Kanter discussed building power through organizational activities.[1] Engaging in activities that are extraordinary, relevant, or visible can enhance power. Engaging in activities that have two of these characteristics is even better. Activities with all three of these characteristics are best, as shown in the story of Elgin.

> **Key: People develop power through activities that are perceived to be extraordinary, relevant, and visible.**

I am reminded of Henri Fayol (1841–1925), the great pioneer of management, who for 30 years was CEO of a successful French coal and metallurgical firm. Fayol began his career as a mining engineer working in a coal mine. The first week on the job a fire broke out in the mine, which happened occasionally in those days.[2] The mining company had to put out the fires and then work to get the mines started up again. This took time, and reduced productivity. Fayol took it upon himself to study the problem of mine fires. No one told him to do this; it just seemed like a problem that needed study. He tackled the problem and over time he found a way to put out fires faster and get the mines back up and running more quickly. His efforts did not go unnoticed, and eventually led him to the top leadership position in the company.

This story about Fayol demonstrates how to build power through activities. Fayol went beyond the requirements of his job, beyond the ordinary day-to-day duties for which he was hired. His effort to solve the problem was extraordinary, and was not in his job description. He succeeded in finding a better solution to the problem. Fayol was an employee who added value. The problem he tackled was relevant, it went directly to the bottom line of the mining business—getting that mine back online. It was visible. I can imagine some superintendent of mines wondering why Mine 17 was up and running so quickly after a fire. Recovering operations quickly would get the attention of higher-ups. Management would take an interest in this young mining engineer, Henri Fayol.

I followed Kanter's advice about activities when I took my position on the faculty at Mount St. Joseph University. At the beginning of my first semester, the academic dean—the leader of all academic activities—addressed the faculty. He said that a particular task force on curriculum issues would be doing what, in his opinion, was the most important work of the year. He added that anyone interested in being on the task force should let him know. I was new. I had to do more than just teach and research, I also had to engage in service. Here was a highly visible task force whose work was very relevant to the core mission of the university. I volunteered. The work was challenging and tiring but rewarding, especially in meeting and developing lasting friendships with other members of the task force. Kanter's advice was not an afterthought. It was the grounding that informed my decision to volunteer. It was a good decision.

Think about your job. You only have so much energy you can give. Where do you put that energy? It's easy to spend our days fighting alligators and to lose track of the fact that our problems could be solved by draining the swamp. What problems or opportunities in your workplace need tackling? You might not be able to handle them tomorrow, but having a mindset that acknowledges that they exist and are workable might lead to action. Even in your daily activities there can be choices. "Hey, we need a volunteer for. . . ." Choose wisely. Some opportunities do not drain the swamp—they drain us. But some increase our visibility in the organization, and bring us into contact with others whom we might not meet otherwise. Whatever your position, you will engage in different activities. Make your choices count.

> **Key: Power is strengthened by strong relationships with people above you, your peers, and people in lower positions.**

Kanter wrote about building power through our alliances with sponsors, peers, and subordinates.[3] All of our relationships with others are power relationships to various degrees. Potentially our power can grow as a result of strong, positive relationships upward, laterally, or down. Some people network well with those above them in the organizations. Others have great peer relationships. Still others are liked or respected by their subordinates. Some people have great relationships at all levels. Strong relationships in all directions build the most power.

Alicia's fine work had caught the eye of Doreen Albans, VP of Operations. Doreen had made a point of monitoring Alicia's progress in the organization, meeting with her occasionally, sharing pointers that can only come from years in the trenches, and—when needed—putting in a good word about Alicia from time to time with the "right people." Alicia understood that Doreen had taken a personal interest in her career and so did Alicia's bosses. Alicia was appreciative of Doreen's interest and worked hard to keep that trust.

Alicia was on a business trip to Los Angeles when her boss called.

"While you are on the coast, we need you to fly up to San Francisco and meet with Jacque Arrows on the Cyldebergen deal. We have to educate him on all that's happened and find out where he stands. He could sink the whole project. See what you can do."

"This will be a tough one," Alicia thought. Arrows was a recluse, but a powerful and influential recluse. Over the next two days repeated phone calls and e-mails to Arrows's office went unanswered. Alicia called her boss.

"Lou, I've done all I can do out here."

"Well," said Lou, "All I can tell you is that getting Arrows' buy-in is important to the VP for Marketing, if you get my drift. Do what you have to do." Lou ended the call.

Alicia thought for a moment and then called Doreen Albans. Alicia explained the situation.

"I'll call you back within the hour," said Albans, and she did. "Meet Mr. Arrows at his residence at 2 p.m. tomorrow. He will be expecting you—and good luck."

Alicia met Arrows the next day and obtained the buy-in her company needed.

Doreen Albans was Alicia's sponsor or mentor. As do many top executives, Doreen always kept an eye out for talent. She had identified Alicia as having high potential, someone to groom for bigger and better positions at the company. Some companies have formal sponsor or mentoring programs to assist with organizational socialization, learning the ropes, and occasionally career guidance.

The more powerful sponsors and mentors are informal; a higher-up takes an interest in furthering the career of someone lower in the pecking order. These sponsors can make a difference in the closed-door discussions about who gets which opportunities. Such sponsors also can cut through red tape or find shortcuts or needed resources.

In the example provided above, Albans pulled a few strings in her informal network and made the important meeting happen; she made Alicia's path easier. Sponsors do this. When Alicia was meeting with Arrows, Alicia was representing Albans. Kanter would say that she had the "reflected power" of her sponsor.[4] A powerful sponsor opens doors; provides opportunities; and simplifies, fortifies, and stands behind your words and deeds.

To have a powerful sponsor can be a Godsend—but take the wrong action once or twice and the relationship could vanish. You benefit from the relationship at the discretion of the sponsor.

So how do you acquire a sponsor? Be outstanding in your job and engage in those activities that are visible, relevant, and extraordinary. Even so, there are no guarantees. In some cases a sponsor could take an interest in you because of some perceived similarity, such as being graduates of the same college or having a shared interest. In other cases there could be connections through family or friends—which you might or might not know about—that incline a superior to sponsor or mentor a lower-level employee. The best executives will be on the lookout for talent. Earn their attention by your performance.

> Seth was the "golden boy." One of ten analysts, he often was away from the office on company business resolving client problems. When he was in the office, he spent much of his time in discussions with senior management.
>
> One day, after Seth returned from a meeting, an administrative assistant dropped by his desk. Reaching into a small trash can, the assistant picked up a yellow sticky note, handed it to Seth, and said, "I thought you might like to know what your peers are doing to you."
>
> The note read, "Seth, please meet Robins at 10 a.m., his office."
>
> Robins was the CFO. The meeting was in ten minutes. If not for the assistant, Seth would have missed the meeting.
>
> Seth was puzzled by what had happened, but then he recalled the reports and documents that he couldn't locate. He was being sabotaged by his peers. The truth was that Seth didn't know his peers. He didn't chat with them much during the workday and he never socialized with them after hours. When he had first taken this job a year ago, several had invited him to join them at a local "watering hole" after work but he had declined. He was too busy. His coworkers didn't know him, either.

Like Seth, I learned the importance of good peer relations the hard way. I recall a time as a young Air Force officer when I was totally involved in my work and did not work at building relationships with my peers. Instead of joining them at the Officers' Club on Friday night, I worked late. I really thought I could do it on my own, that I didn't need them. But I was wrong, very wrong. When I needed help from my peers, they cooperated but did so slowly and half-heartedly. No one works alone in our organizations. I had the good sense to recognize my mistake and I worked hard to turn things around. I did but it was difficult and took time.

Don't be too busy for your peers. They can make you or break you. The workplace is full of dependencies. We need each other for information, for help. We build peer relations through interactions that enable us to find common interests. Peers often build power with each other by doing each other favors. Building relationships with subordinates and direct reports is equally important. Sometimes, however, it might just happen by doing the right thing.

Major Reynolds would miss the Chief. Chief Barnes had been his right hand through good and bad. Barnes had risen to the top enlisted rank in the Air Force, Chief Master Sergeant, but he had never lost his humility. Now he was retiring.

"How can I tell the Chief how much he has meant to me?" Reynolds wondered. "Especially someone like the Chief who likes neither recognition nor acclaim, although highly deserving of both." It occurred to Reynolds that actions speak louder than words.

It was late on a Friday afternoon, the end of a long workweek.

"Chief, how about joining me for a drink over at Ted's Place?" asked Major Reynolds. Reynolds knew that Barnes frequented Ted's Place nearly every Friday after work.

"Glad to, Major. It has been a tough week."

So the Chief and the Major walked into Ted's—which on this particular Friday night was packed with the Chief's best buddies and many friends, mostly enlisted members of the Air Force. Major Reynolds had invited them all to a surprise party for the Chief. The bar and buffet for all were courtesy of Major Reynolds, who footed the bill out of his own pocket.

Before the night was over, he took a moment to say to the Chief, "I just wanted you to know how much I appreciate all that you have done."

It was a good party and a special evening.

The rest was unexpected. The next Monday, Sergeant Waylon came into see Major Reynolds.

"Sir, I just want you to know that all of the enlisted were impressed with what you did for the Chief last week. We just don't expect that from officers anymore."

The word of what Major Reynolds had done for the Chief spread rapidly among the enlisted both in and out of the organization. Major Reynolds had good relations with subordinates in the past but after what he did for the Chief, they were absolutely superb.

Never underestimate those who work for you and their peers. If you are a manager or supervisor, you know your success depends on them. Even if you are not a manager, your effectiveness can be affected very strongly by your relationships with others.

Key: People differ greatly in their abilities to use power appropriately and effectively.

It is not enough to build power, you also must know how and when to use it. There are people who are very effective at using power and there are those who do not have a clue. John Kotter found that managers who were most effective at using power had some characteristics in common.[5] His findings underscore principles in using power, regardless of whether you are a manager.

People who are good at using power are sensitive to the norms, roles, and culture of their workplace. They do not use power in ways that conflict with norms about power, that are inconsistent with their perceived roles, or that are out of sync with their organizational culture.

Roger was excited to begin his second career. After a successful 25 years climbing the corporate ladder, Roger was changing gears. He had accepted a position at a local community college as head of the Department of Business.

He soon learned that the professors in his department did things differently from workers in the "real world"—and much of it Roger didn't care for at all. He decreed that everybody must be at work by 8 a.m. unless they were teaching night classes. He expected them to be in the office all day unless they had school-related business elsewhere. Roger wanted to know where staff members were at all times.

When Olivia showed up one day at 8:30 a.m., Roger chastised her so loudly it could be heard throughout the department. Roger had started a second career, but he had much to learn about his new workplace.

Roger failed to realize that what were acceptable uses of departmental power in his old corporate job were not acceptable in his new academic position. Autocratic, strong uses of power were common in his old organization but are rare in an academic institution. Here, departmental power was used more collaboratively, sometimes even discreetly.

Organizations vary in what's acceptable and what's not in using power. Picking up on this is part of organizational socialization. You cannot use power the same way in every job and every organization. Observe others and adjust accordingly.

Those who best use power do so maturely. They do not use their power impulsively or vindictively—those who do so run great risks.

Jaclyn admired her boss, Mr. Harlow. One day at a staff meeting, however, Mr. Harlow seemed upset and made an odd request.

"Petersen over in Accounting has been jerking me around. If anybody comes across anything where he might be seen unfavorably, let me know."

A few days later a memo from Petersen landed on Jaclyn's desk. Reading it, she realized that Petersen had made an error. Not the kind of error that simply had to be corrected, but rather the type of error that—if exposed—would be like a pie in Petersen's face. Because of the nature of her job, Jaclyn was the only person who knew—or would know—about the error. Then she remembered Mr. Harlow's request. What should she do?

The next day she dropped by Mr. Harlow's office. "I thought you might like to see this," Jaclyn said.

Harlow pushed his chair back from his desk, leaned back, read the memo, and then laughed heartily.

"Thanks, Jaclyn. This is great." Then he put the memo into a desk drawer.

Jaclyn smiled. She knew Mr. Harlow would never use the memo to embarrass Petersen. It just wasn't his style. But if he did, Jaclyn would find out about it in the course of her job. Mr. Harlow never used the memo.

Jaclyn perceived correctly that Harlow really was not vindictive. She had observed him for two years and had learned much. Harlow was the most influential manager with whom she had ever worked, but he had never used his influence in ways that went beyond the boundaries of what was appropriate and proper—unlike some managers Jaclyn had known. Use power with reason, not with emotion. Do not use power to get revenge or to hurt others.

Across the course of a career, the best users of power seek out positions from which they can increase their power. Once established, they seek positions with greater opportunities. Even at the entry level not all jobs are created equal, not even jobs with the same title and in the same organization. Some positions have more potential for learning the business, for recognition, for advancement, for developing power. A young loan officer might be offered a choice of the same position at several branches of the same bank. Most likely, one of these will offer greater opportunities than the others. Who is serviced by the branch? Who is the branch manager? How is each branch doing as compared with the others? Opportunities rarely are the same. Would you rather be the first person in a new position or be a replacement? Would you rather replace a manager who did poorly or one who walked on water? Would you rather work at a position central to the mission of your company, such as in operations, or one that is less central, such as community relations? Would you rather have a position that is safe and secure, or one that involves some risk? Would you rather be responsible for resources critical to your organization's bottom line or support the people who use those resources? Answers to such questions shape careers and the development of power.

Decoding the workplace requires having insight into the power-related processes around you and knowledge about who has power, how much, and how they use it. All of the power-building activities discussed in this chapter and the previous chapter can provide clues about the power of people around you. In *Managing with Power*, Jeffrey Pfeffer of the Stanford Business School suggested looking at who controls resources, who controls information, and who has formal authority.[6] Some powerful people occupy positions of authority in the organization. Others do not have such positions but informally have great influence among coworkers. Occasionally, a person will rise to a position of legitimate authority—such as a manager in a company—and have no idea how to use or build power.

> "You won't believe whose down at the copier—it's Mr. Wallace."
>
> Mr. Wallace, a middle manager earning a six-figure salary, stood by the copier for the entire afternoon. He looked at everything that was being copied to be sure it was for company use, not personal business. He counted copies, often questioning people about why this or that many copies.

Rosabeth Moss Kanter described powerless people like Mr. Wallace.[7] They have legitimate power but little else—no idea how to build their power. They very often are micromanagers who strictly enforce rules and policies. They show little discretion to subordinates, are very controlling, and sometimes even are coercive. They play it safe and go by the book. You might have met some of them. You might work for one of them. They depend totally on the authority of their position to demand compliance from others. The power-building activities we have discussed are not part of their repertoires. These people are to be avoided if possible.

Observe the workplace and you will see the dynamics of power at play. People growing their power; people using power effectively and ineffectively. Ally yourself with people who acquire and successfully use power at whatever level. These are people who can make a positive difference in the lives and fortunes of others. Better yet, be such a person.

Part VI: Outcomes

CHAPTER THIRTEEN

Job Satisfaction, Conflict, and Stress: What's Good, What's Not, What's Hidden

Hannah and Andrea were sisters who worked for different companies. Hannah loved her job. She did not have to work very hard; she took her time, worked at her own pace; no hurry. Hannah often stopped what she was doing and just surfed the Internet. No one noticed or seemed to care. She enjoyed chatting with her coworkers and her boss. Her boss was laid back and joked a lot. There were a few people in her work group who stayed very busy but not Hannah.

Andrea did not like her job. She did not enjoy going to work in the morning. She did not like her supervisor. Her boss thought she was a slacker, even though she wasn't. On her most recent performance appraisal, Andrea's boss told her he wasn't sure the job was a good fit for her. Andrea was silent but she disagreed. "Nothing wrong with the job," she thought, "I just need a better supervisor." She had thought about leaving but knew that the job market would be tough. So she decided she'd show the boss and everyone else just what she could do. Andrea upped her game and worked even harder.

Hannah had high job satisfaction but was not very productive. Andrea had low job satisfaction but was very productive. So is the happy worker a more productive worker? Nearly everyone thinks so. Keep the workers happy. The problem is that this common-sense idea that happy workers always are more productive is wrong.[1] This is one finding that most people find puzzling, but the research evidence is clear and overwhelming.

Job satisfaction and performance probably are the most studied concepts in the history of organizational behavior.[2] In 1935, Robert Hoppock published the first comprehensive study of job satisfaction.[3] By the early 1990s there were more than 12,000 studies that had examined some aspect of job satisfaction.[4] Hundreds of studies are conducted every year. The findings about job satisfaction and performance are counterintuitive. The happy worker is not necessarily a more productive worker. In statistical terms there is only a small correlation between job satisfaction and individual performance.

Why so many studies? To try to determine when and where job satisfaction might be related to performance. To study which aspects of job satisfaction might be related to performance. To study the effects of job dissatisfaction. To look at job satisfaction and job dissatisfaction from every angle and possibility. Does this mean that companies should not be concerned about whether their employees like their jobs? Of course they should be concerned. It affects an organization's bottom line and other things, as we shall see.

> **Key: People who are happier in their jobs are not necessarily more productive, but they are more likely to show up for work and not leave the organization.**

Employee turnover is costly. Regardless of the level of the employee in the organization, there are costs to recruit and train. These costs increase depending upon the employee's level within the company. An unhappy worker is more likely to leave an organization or not show up for work. Although the relationship of job satisfaction to performance is not as strong as most would expect, the relationships between job dissatisfaction and turnover and absenteeism are very strong.

Job satisfaction is an attitude. Understanding attitudes is important to understanding yourself and others. An attitude is how you feel about something, some belief, either positive or negative. Beliefs are cognitive, things we have learned. I see a little animal that says "meow" and has whiskers. It's a cat. That's the belief level. But "I love cats" is an attitude. Conversely, I might dislike cats—which still is an attitude. We all have attitudes; they develop across our life experiences. Some are rooted deep in one's childhood. Others were formed last week, or even yesterday. And they all can change.

We evaluate our beliefs to form attitudes; our attitudes influence our intentions; and our intentions are related to our behaviors. The relationship between intentions and behaviors varies from very weak in many cases, to very strong in others.[5] Core values and core beliefs produce stronger attitudes, intentions, and—often—behavior. A person with strong religious beliefs will be more likely to have behaviors consistent with those beliefs.

People have attitudes about many things. To understand others in the workplace, however, the most important attitude is job satisfaction—how a person feels about their job. Do the people around you enjoy their jobs? Does it vary? How do you feel about your job? Working in an environment where people like their jobs is very different from an environment where people do not.

Knowing some of the factors that lead to job satisfaction or dissatisfaction should help you understand yourself and others. All of those studies of job satisfaction provide a good picture of the factors that affect how we feel about our job. Ed Locke summarized the literature in 1976 and his findings are still valid.[6]

Travis, the owner of a successful plumbing company, sat is his office watching the snow fall outside the window. He had several crews who would be busy today repairing burst pipes. He remembered the early days when he and a buddy were starting to grow the business. Travis was glad he would not have to be out working in the cold today, and he appreciated his employees who were doing so.

Being a plumber was never boring—there always was some new wrinkle that you hadn't seen. Solving a plumbing problem and making things work sometimes was challenging but it always was satisfying. Travis could not imagine what work was like for his brother, who sat in an office all day pushing papers. "At least," Travis thought, "I see the results of our work."

Travis was proud of the company he had built, the employees to whom he gave a livelihood. He knew that his company was well-respected in the community. Just four years ago, his company had received the Torch Award for Workplace Ethics from the Better Business Bureau. He thought, "Starting and building this business was one of the best decisions I ever made."

The work we do has a big influence on how we feel about our job. Travis saw plumbing as a challenging job in a good sense. Without challenges—especially mental challenges—a job can be boring. In the early years on a plumbing job, Travis was personally responsible for taking care of the plumbing issues. He was good at it. We like jobs that we can do well. Travis could see the project from beginning to end. Being able to see the "whole piece of work" or at least see how your part fits into the whole is important. Some companies provide opportunities for employees to interact with those who benefit from their products or services so employees can see how their activities contribute to the whole enterprise.[7]

Just as he was a good plumber, Travis was a good small business owner. He found growing and running the business to be very interesting and meaningful. He took pride in his company, even before receiving the Torch Award. Travis remembered well working important jobs on cold days, but he did not miss the physical strains that came with some of those hard jobs. For Travis, the nature of the work was a big part of his job satisfaction. Is your work interesting? Do you know how your work contributes? Are you challenged? Is it meaningful?

One might think that the amount we are paid would be a big factor in job satisfaction. For some, perhaps, it is. For most, though, the key is fairness. Do I perceive that I am receiving a fair wage? If not, then pay can be a source of dissatisfaction, even turnover. Fairness also is the key to promotions and most company policies. People want to be treated fairly.

Physical working conditions are only major factors in satisfaction if they are extreme. I have visited attractive offices but one that I visited years ago really sticks in my mind. It was located in Crystal City, a neighborhood in Arlington, Virginia. It was an enormous corner office very high in an office building, and two sides were all glass. The view was a panorama of Reagan National Airport, the Jefferson Memorial, the Tidal Basin, the National Mall, Washington Monument, Lincoln Memorial, and the Potomac. Wow! How one could get any work done in this office I do not know. It was breathtaking. I would want to just watch planes take off and land for hours.

On the other hand, I once worked on an Air Force base in an office that had formerly been a dormitory. Our offices were in a basement. Every few months we'd arrive at work to wet floors. We never knew exactly what happened or how the floors got wet. Once a month, people from Bioenvironmental Services came to our offices. They placed a canister on a file cabinet that periodically throughout the day made a short "psssh" sound. None of this was a problem until one day the Bioenvironmental technician came into our offices wearing a mask. We figured he was joking but we followed up. Bioenvironmental Services was testing asbestos levels. The data collected indicated that our air was fine—but had we been in Europe, where the standards were tougher, the air would not have been deemed safe. With some active campaigning up the hierarchy chain, we got our offices moved.

The people with whom you work also are major factors—especially your supervisor. If you do not get along with your boss, your workplace life can be miserable. As a consultant I conducted organizational feedback studies, taking snapshots of climate and morale. If I found an office with high job dissatisfaction, usually my first hypothesis would be that there were human-relations issues with the supervisor. Most of the time this was the case. Replacing a supervisor who has poor human-relations skills with a supervisor who has good skills can be a quick fix to increase job satisfaction.

Research shows that one of the most powerful influences on satisfaction is easily overlooked, and that simply is giving credit where credit is due. Most people want to be recognized for their efforts and their accomplishments. Verbal recognition, a word here or there, goes a long way for human relations.

There also are individual differences in job satisfaction, just because of the way people are. Some people are easygoing and seem to be satisfied under a wide range of organizational settings. Other people are constant complainers.

> Tammy was upset and talking, as usual.
> "It's 12:32 and Sherry still is not back from lunch. She's two minutes late. She was supposed to be back at 12:30. She does this all the time. She just takes advantage of the boss and everyone else. I don't think it's fair. If I were two minutes late, Mr. Simpson would give me the 'what for.' I don't think the way he treats us is fair anyway. I never leave early or come in late. He probably doesn't even notice. Someday he's gonna notice who does the work around here 'cause I won't be here. That'll teach him. Here comes Little Miss Late Again."

Tammy probably would not be happy anywhere. In a lifetime of work, most of us will know a few "Tammys." Although Tammy's behavior might be annoying at times, things are much worse when there exists significant interpersonal conflict.

Key: Interpersonal conflicts occur in the workplace; some escalate, negatively affecting others, and might remain unresolved.

People working together naturally will have some disagreements. Conflict is a characteristic of the workplace. Conflict can be helpful, even functional, clarifying goals or determining who gets which resources. More often though, we tend to think of conflict as not helpful, as dysfunctional, and not aiding the activities or tasks at hand—perhaps even making work accomplishment more difficult. My guess is that when we think about conflict in the workplace, we tend to think about interpersonal conflicts. People disagreeing and that disagreement escalated—often poisoning the relationship and affecting people around those directly involved.

Shawn and Blake co-founded a small business. They had been fraternity brothers in college and still enjoyed each other's company. The business did well and grew in size and revenue for several years. But as their business grew, disagreements became more frequent. Shawn favored steady, slow growth staying within their means and incurring no debt. Blake saw a lot of potential now. He wanted to take more risks, take on more debt, and expand rapidly. This basic disagreement started carrying over to every decision, every interaction. Shawn perceived that Blake was reckless and irresponsible. Blake wondered why Shawn went into business with him if he didn't have the guts to seize opportunities.

The early days of having a beer together after work and golfing on weekends turned into two people who now spoke to each other as little as possible. When they did interact, it was not pleasant. Each called the other names behind his back. The employees of the small business were miserable. Shawn would tell them one thing; then Blake would tell them something else. Finally Blake had had enough. He told Shawn exactly what he thought of him and announced that he was selling his half of the company. He was fed up.

The evolving interpersonal conflict of Shawn and Blake typifies the potential progression of such conflicts. Louis Pondy described this progression more than 50 years ago.[8] The possibility for conflict always exists. It perhaps is not apparent but can be latent in the conditions of the workplace or organization. It is natural that Shawn and Blake would disagree from time to time. At some point, one or both of them started seeing the other differently. They could be on the same page but because they misunderstood each other they had no idea that their positions were similar. They began to perceive fundamental differences in what they each believed about the business and what to do for its future. As these differences became clearer and stronger, Shawn and Blake slowly became uncomfortable around each other and grew apart. Shawn felt anxious about what was happening in his relationship with Blake. Blake more often was angry that he had chosen Shawn as a business partner. Finally, the conflict grew so bad that they verbally assaulted each other and made it hard for the employees to know whose directions to follow. If they did what Shawn said, Blake would tell them the opposite. At no point did Shawn or Blake consider turning to a third party for resolution, to repair the relationship, to move forward together again. Instead, Blake sold his half and started another business.

Workplace conditions lead to disagreements, real or imagined (latent conflict). We perceive conflicts with another or others, real or imagined (perceived conflict). Then we personalize the conflict, however, such that we can have intrusive thoughts and negative emotions, we become tense or anxious (felt conflict). The conflict that had originated only in one's mind starts to take its toll on the body. Anyone who has been in a close relationship with others probably has experienced this at some time. A good solution at this point is to talk it out. "Here's what is troubling me. Here's how I feel." "What do you think?" "How can we fix this? What can we do?" I think most of us experience these types of conflicts in our homes, with our neighbors, with our friends, and in the workplace.

Unresolved though, interpersonal conflicts can escalate to their most destructive phase (manifest conflict) where the actions of one or both parties negatively impact the workplace and the organization. Employees might become verbally abusive, sabotage each other's work, spread rumors, or even assassinate the character of the other person, or they might just give the other person "the cold shoulder," or "the silent treatment."

> Felicia and Martha shared a workspace, and sat just five feet apart. Felicia did not like Martha and Martha did not like Felicia. They had very different styles and, to their knowledge, no common interests. It had been that way since Felicia was hired and started working beside Martha. At first they expressed a few pleasantries, such as "Nice day," but said little more. One day Martha made a comment about Felicia's work. Felicia exploded, told Martha off, and then shut up. For the next 20 years Martha and Felicia worked beside each other but they never spoke to each other again.

As hard as it might be to believe this, such things do happen. The silent treatment is the most pervasive form of manifest conflict that I have witnessed in my professional life. People have a conflict, it escalates, and they never speak again although they see each other daily. It is not a fun way to work. In the extreme, physical violence can occur. The best supervisors act immediately when an interpersonal conflict moves to the level of manifest conflict. Unfortunately, resolving conflicts is not easy or pleasant; but it is part of the boss's job, even if it is hard to step up to the plate.

Your relations with coworkers significantly affect your job satisfaction and dissatisfaction. The people in your workplace could be like a second family—be that good or bad. Poor relations in the workplace, and especially interpersonal conflict, can be exceedingly stressful—they even can affect your health.

Key: You can see aspects of stress in the workplace, but significant effects of stress often are hidden.

Job dissatisfaction has organizational and individual costs. We have discussed turnover and absenteeism, and the individual costs can be even greater.

Judd Turner ate, lived, and breathed his job. A midlevel marketing analyst in his early 40s, he threw himself into every undertaking. He was pleased when Wallace, the Senior VP for Marketing, selected him to develop the marketing plan for a new product that was anticipated to be the company's profit leader within three years. The challenges were enormous; the expectations for success were high. Turner knew this project would make or break his career.

For four months Turner worked on the project nearly every waking minute. He went to bed thinking about the plan and woke up with it on his mind. Except for sleep, his effort was 24/7. His wife, Gina, had never seen him work this much or this hard. Slowly his behavior changed. He grew emotionally distant; bottles of scotch disappeared more quickly. Gina thought, "I will be so thankful when this is over and I can have my husband back." But this was not to be.

Turner kept the Senior VP for Marketing in the loop as the plan developed. The Senior VP had nothing but praise for Turner's work. Finally he told Turner, "This is brilliant. Absolutely brilliant. I think we're ready to take this to the CEO. Great work, Judd."

The meeting with the CEO and senior staff was arranged. Turner presented the plan. But the meeting did not go as anticipated. From the start, it was clear the CEO did not understand how the plan would achieve the marketing goals. Turner did his best but the CEO just didn't get it. Turner kept waiting for the Senior VP for Marketing to jump in and help him out. He knew Wallace understood the plan and thought it was great.

Finally the CEO, exasperated, said, "OK, that's enough. I don't see anything here worth pursuing. This plan just stinks. What do you think, Wallace?" Without hesitating, the Senior VP for Marketing replied, "Yes, sir. Pretty smelly. I should have given Turner more guidance. We'll regroup and get someone else on it immediately."

Turner felt shock; absolute shock. Turner could barely take a breath. His superior had not supported him. He had, in fact, betrayed him. As Turner walked back to his office, replaying the past few minutes in his mind, he felt as if the air was being squeezed out of him. Months of giving everything to the company, years of dedicated service—and it was over. It was all over. All he felt was pain, emptiness, failure. He couldn't breathe. He couldn't breathe. Turner opened the window in his office on the 23rd floor—and stepped through it into eternity.

News of Turner's suicide stunned the organization. Those who knew him were incredulous. Turner was so level-headed, such a normal guy. What could have happened? The signs were there—the lack of sleep; the alcohol abuse; the emotional detachment. Turner was in the most stressful job of his life—and it got to him. He didn't manage the stress. He was stressed out long before the fateful meeting with the CEO; but when his superior did not back him—and instead left him standing all alone—the thread that held Turner to reality snapped. A darkness deep and vast came over him and took him away.

The consequences of dysfunctional stress can creep upon us. Over a career you will work with coworkers who have a variety of stress-related ailments—from backaches, to hypertension, to headaches, to depression. Sometimes you will know about these ailments but other times you will not. Work-related stress can play out in our private lives, such as through drug abuse, both legal and illegal. You might develop stress-related problems yourself. Some people even die from stress-related coronary diseases. The Japanese have a word for death from work, "karoshi." Estimates of the annual cost of stress for U.S. organizations range as high as $300 billion.

A previous chapter discussed sources of stress associated with role conflicts (interrole, intrasender, intersender, role ambiguity, role overload). In the workplace, other sources of stress might be easy to identify, such as coworkers or supervisors. But others might not be visible. In many organizations, for example, there exist stressful norms about how long a person should work.

> Miguel was a great employee. His individual productivity was almost twice the average worker in his department. He worked smart and he worked fast. At 5 p.m., when the work day was over, Miguel left for home. Usually he was the only one in his office who left. Occasionally there would be a few remarks made once he was gone.

> "What a slacker."
> "No wonder we end up doing so much work."
> "Can't he see we're still here?"
> "I don't know who he thinks he is."

> Miguel's coworkers would continue to work until 6 or 7 p.m., or even later. They left after their boss had departed for the evening.

"Too much to do and not enough time to do it" is a popular expression. Think about it. Why do we live our lives this way? Do we really want people to "work" longer hours than necessary? Do we really have to put in "face time" to get ahead? What is the cost to individuals? To the organization? Miguel probably was getting a good workout at the gym while his coworkers were still at the office. But will Miguel get the recognition he deserves as a productive employee? Will it lead to bonuses? It really depends. There are offices across America where the unwritten rule is that you do not go home before the boss does, no matter how long the boss works.

Research indicates that a small amount of stress can improve performance. You might feel that you do your best work when you are under a lot of stress. Beyond some point, however, performance goes downhill. It is at this point—when productivity begins to fall—that you have the least insight into your own stress. We are not good at recognizing that we are under too much stress. Others are better judges than we are. They see the symptoms before we do. They see the increased irritability, the decreased productivity, the coworker who bickers or complains more than usual.

People are stressed by different factors. We call these "stressors." The stressors you perceive in your environment can be very different from those of someone else in the same environment. These stressors you perceive affect you psychologically. You might experience frustration. Frustration can come from something blocking your goal, such as the car in front of you that is still sitting there even though the traffic light turned green five seconds ago. Or you might experience anxiety. The anxiety could be real, for example, if you have just lost your job. Or the anxiety could stem from something that is not real, and is just imagined, such as the fear you might lose your job when, in fact, that will not happen. These frustrations and anxieties have physical effects on your body. The resulting psychological and physical strains can range from small to debilitating or, as mentioned, even can lead to death.

My first vivid encounter with stress was when I was a senior in high school. Wrestling practice had ended. Time to head home. In the Piedmont of North Carolina, the January air was crisp. It was twilight. I walked out of the gym and toward my car. Well, to be precise, it was actually our family car. But my dad bought it on my 16th birthday and told me privately that it was really mine—and what a car! A '59 Chevy Impala, black with red interior, twin antenna on the rear. At 70 mph it wanted to fly, but didn't have wings.

As I walked toward the Chevy, I noticed my left hand beginning to twitch, then shake, and then my right; and the shaking was increasing. I started to feel sick. I wanted to vomit. I was closer to the outside wall of the gym building than to the car. I walked over and leaned my back against the building. Then my legs collapsed. I slumped beside the gym, shaking all over, crying uncontrollably. No one else was outside. No one saw me.

After a minute or two I regained my composure. I made my way to the car, drove home on country roads, and told my parents what had happened. They called our family doctor who said simply, "Run a tub of hot water and have Johnny sit in it for an hour." That did the trick. Afterwards I felt fine. To this day if I take a bath instead of taking a shower, my wife will ask how I am feeling.

I did not understand what was happening at the time. Looking back it's easy to see that my experience was a consequence of dysfunctional stress. I was under great pressures, as most teenagers are at some point. No one in my family had ever gone to college. There was no money to help me and I understood that. I was competing for a congressional appointment to the U.S. Air Force Academy, but the odds were against me 50 to 1. The girl of my dreams was dating my best friend and the girl I was dating was in love with another guy. Stress got to me. Even though I was in great shape as a wrestler, stress knocked me up against the wall. It shook me. It said "enough is enough."

Many years later, I experienced stress in the extreme. About a month after an auto accident, I started experiencing pains as if I were about to have a heart attack. My blood pressure climbed to precariously dangerous levels. I became very sick. My doctor ordered tests and prescribed medications but my "sickness" continued. My body and mind ached. Six weeks passed. I did not know how long I could endure this illness. One night, on my way home from class, I drove through the intersection where the accident occurred. It was a rainy evening like it was on the night of the accident. I started shaking. I felt totally helpless. I drove the few remaining blocks to our home, lay down beside my wife, and cried for 20 minutes as she held me. Then everything was fine. All my symptoms disappeared. Post-traumatic stress. I had read about it and written about it but I had never experienced it. There are powerful memories in our bodies that we might or might not have access to without professional help. Stress can kill.

We are creatures of the savanna. We are conditioned to fight or flee. When we are in a dangerous situation, chemicals are released into the bloodstream to give us the energy to run or to engage. When the boss you don't like enters into your office, those same chemicals flow, but you can't run and you can't fight. This fight-or-flight mechanism is an underlying source of wear and tear on the body.[9] It happens throughout our days in stressful situations and without our ever noticing. Then one day we have a headache, a backache, or other manifestation. This General Adaptive Syndrome that served us well in our ancestral past takes a toll on us in modern workplaces.

How well people around you manage their workplace stress depends on many factors. To what degree does the company encourage wellness and good health? I tell my students that the key to stress reduction is three things: 1. Exercise. 2. Exercise. 3. Exercise. Even if it is just walking 30 minutes three times a week. Reducing stress has to be a commitment or it will not happen. Learning to take the time to relax can be difficult. For example, small business owners might feel that they cannot risk taking a vacation. Then there are the workers who feel that they just have to work, who miss being at work, and who even curtail vacations to get back on the job sooner. Others are just so wrapped up in the day-to-day business of life that they have no time for themselves. There is so much to fill our time that, for many of us, it takes great effort to make time to relax.

The sources of job dissatisfaction can be sources of stress—even significant stress. If we are more knowledgeable about stress, perhaps we can avoid stressful situations or resolve stress that might occur. Job satisfaction might not be significantly related to job performance but it is related to something more important—life satisfaction.[10] People who are happy in their jobs are more likely to be happy in their lives overall.

Erdman Palmore studied longevity. In 1969, in *The Gerontologist,* Palmore and his associates reported the results of a longitudinal study.[11] They studied people over many years late in life. At first they interviewed and gathered data from more than 200 people who were 60 to 64 years of age. Fifteen years later they checked to see how many of these people had died. For those still living, the researchers estimated their remaining years using actuarial tables. The question Palmore was trying to answer was "What is the best predictor of how long a person will live? Is it health activities? Education? Occupation? Tobacco use?" The results were stunning. The single best predictor was job satisfaction. Those people 15 years before who reported that they felt useful and were doing meaningful work were the most likely to live longer. Job satisfaction in the latter part of one's work life was highly correlated with the longevity of that life.

People around you in the workplace probably vary in their satisfaction with their jobs, and their satisfaction with their lives. You will see conflicts, both functional and dysfunctional. You will see interpersonal conflicts at various stages. You will probably experience the effects of stress. Choose how you respond to the workplace. Given a chance to lead, set a healthy standard in the hours you work, and the management of your own stress. Be a role model.

Meaning: What Is Important to Me Might Not Be Important to You—Making Sense of Our Lives and the Workplace

Thomas was the Outstanding Graduate in finance from his university. He obtained a plum job working for a hedge fund at a prestigious company. The hours were long, but Thomas excelled at every undertaking. After one year, he quit. In that one year he had earned $1.2 million, including bonuses. Thomas enjoyed the details of finance but he did not enjoy the culture of the hedge fund. His life was not about just making as much money as possible. With good investing he could live a comfortable life using the money he pocketed from working at the hedge fund.

Thomas found a nonprofit company dedicated to economic development in Africa. The nonprofit needed an expert in finance to work with developing regional enterprises. The pay was low but adequate. Thomas liked the idea of using his knowledge to elevate the economic condition of Africans in need of help. He had been brought up to serve others, and this was a great way to do it. He had found his calling.

Thomas was fortunate. He had enough money to pursue what he really wanted to do. His life took on a new meaning. Viktor Frankl, a survivor of the Nazi concentration camp at Auschwitz, wrote powerfully about man's search for meaning.[1] He viewed the search for meaning as the primary motivation in life. He wrote that one of the ways we can find meaning, our purpose, is through our work.

Key: People differ as to what is most important in their lives, and these differences can be revealing.

Our motivation and our needs vary from situation to situation, but there are themes that run through our lives. These themes reveal what is important to us, what is most meaningful. Sometimes as we move through life we might not have a clue about what is important. Other times it will be clear. As others discuss their lives and their choices, you might see patterns of meaning. These patterns can help decode workplace behaviors.

In 1955, the American Telephone and Telegraph Company (AT&T) committed to a longitudinal study of its managers, a study that would assess individuals over the course of 20 years.[2] Thus began the famous "Management Progress Study" which studied AT&T managers, who at that time were mostly white and male. Years later, AT&T conducted similar research that included women managers and managers from minority groups. Both studies used the assessment center method in which managers were evaluated many different ways, such as via simulations, paper-and-pencil tests, personality inventories, and interviews. One method was an interview with a psychologist in which the manager just talked about his life. These interviews lasted two to four hours. In the first study, the eminent psychologist Joseph Rychlak analyzed detailed notes from more than 350 interviews. What emerged were nine life themes.[3] Although these themes might fluctuate in importance over a lifetime, each manager had a predominant pattern of meaning that emerged in conversation, a pattern reflected in priorities and interests.

People for whom work was the true center of their lives had an "occupational" life theme. They talked mainly about their work and getting ahead. Other managers were more interested in self-development and sought educational opportunities. They read more and engaged in many physical activities and health pursuits. Rychlak labeled these managers as having an "ego-functional" life theme.

Some managers were occupied with accumulating wealth, property, and other possessions. People with this "financial-acquisitive" theme desired symbols of their success. They wanted the recognition that comes from "living well" and enjoying nice things. Other managers were more interested in where they lived than how they lived. A "locale-residential" life theme often surfaced in the interviews. These managers liked their city, their community, or their part of the state. To live where they lived was what they wanted most.

Managers heavily involved in community activities of a nonreligious nature, or serving the nation in the National Guard, Reserves, and other such organizations, characterized the "service" life theme. Managers heavily involved in religious activities or expressing humanistic values indicated a "religious-humanism" theme. For many, enjoying their hobbies, going to movies, or socializing occupied their time. For managers with a "recreational-social" life theme, work was just a means to an end.

Rychlak divided family relations into two themes. Managers with a "marital-familial" theme talked mostly about their spouse and children, and to some degree their in-laws. Managers with a "parental-familial" theme talked more about their parents, brothers, sisters, and old friends.

Following is a conversation among nine coworkers. I have identified the life theme that each coworker appears to be revealing. Over time, with more conversations and observed workplace behaviors, we would have a better idea if these indeed are the major life themes for each individual.

Employees from the office were enjoying some brews after a long week's work. The conversation turned to weekend plans.

"Well, guess I'll be back at the office tomorrow. Got a project to finish. But I really don't mind. You know, I really love what I do. I think I could work for this company for a long time." (Occupational)

"You might but you'll never get rich working here. I'll be moving to a better paying job one of these days." (Financial-acquisitive)

Another coworker chimed in, "Hey, money's no big deal to me. It's enough. I just love living in this part of the country. The weather's perfect. Another great weekend." (Locale-residential)

Still another said, "Yeah, I love all the biking trails. Getting buff. I'll be out there at 6 a.m. Probably do 100 miles this weekend." (Ego-functional)

"While you're doing your 100 miles, I'll be on a campout with a local scout troop. Once an Eagle, always an Eagle." (Service)

"I didn't know you were an Eagle Scout. Me too. But I think I take more pride in my God and Country Award. Not a lot of people have that one. And I think it helped me get my act together." (Religious-humanism)

"Sounds like you guys have big plans. I'm glad the weather looks good. I'm taking the husband and the kids to the zoo." (Marital-familial)

"Well my house is going to be a zoo. My mom and dad are coming in tomorrow for the weekend. My brothers are driving down to hang out. But it'll be fun" (Parental-familial)

"All of you have way too much to do. I'm just gonna chill, sit around the pool, and go over to Terry's party Saturday night. My weekend is lookin' sweet." (Recreational-social)

Rychlak used the term "life theme" or "lifestyle." Most of his life themes sound academic. In the best-selling book, *The 7 Habits of Highly Effective People*, Stephen Covey conveyed pretty much the same ideas but in more popular language. Instead of life themes, he discussed "centers" or "centeredness," stating, "Each of us has a center, though we usually don't recognize it as such."[4] Covey's centers were spouse, family, money, work, possessions, pleasure, friend, enemy, church, self-centered, or principle centered. Given a list of Rychlak's life themes and Covey's centers, it is easy to match them. Only enemy-centered seems unique to Covey.

My guess is that you already have thought of friends or family whose lifestyle fits into one of these themes or centers. I have childhood friends who live only a few miles from where they grew up. They love the area or living near their families. My dad was born and raised in the Piedmont area of North Carolina. After he came back from the Korean War, he was stationed briefly in Monterey, California. He was discharged and returned to the Tar Heel State. Decades later I visited Monterey while doing some consulting. I was overwhelmed with the beauty of Monterey Bay and Carmel. I called my father. "Dad, this place is so beautiful. Why didn't you just settle here?" After a short pause, he answered: "I missed my home." My dad could not leave the red dirt of the Piedmont.

Ann Howard and Douglas Bray's report of the AT&T study, *Managerial Lives in Transition*, is the definitive study of who gets ahead in organizations, who reaches the top. Life theme analyses figured prominently in the study's results. Not surprisingly, managers having the highest scores on the occupational life theme—both men and women—advanced fast and far. In the first several years the differences among managers were small but sometime around the fourth year, occupational life theme scores started to move apart. By year seven, the occupational life theme corresponded to the highest managerial level eventually attained. Those with the highest scores were headed to the higher levels, AT&T Levels 5–6. Those with the lowest scores were destined to stay at Level 1. In most organizations, those who "eat, live, and breathe their jobs" are more likely to rise to the top.

Rachel and Jenna were good friends who worked for the same global company.

"Rachel, I've been thinking about my future. I think I'm going to stay with this company. I've got an excellent sponsor who says there could be some big opportunities ahead. I'm enjoying my work and I'm good at it. I might just lean in a little more, work a little harder, and see how far I can go. Someone has to break the glass ceiling."

"Well, I wish you luck. I enjoy this company and my work, too, but it's not my life. Adam and I are starting to talk about marriage and children. I admire women who can do it all but I really don't think I am one of them."

Years passed. Jenna lived her job, broke the glass ceiling, and became CEO. Rachel remained her best friend, married, and raised a family. Both were happy.

Jenna and Rachel each found their purpose, their central meaning. Both achieved success. How do you define success? Do you know your purpose? Perhaps it has not yet emerged, been found, or been made clear. In a 2012 best-seller, Clayton Christensen, a Harvard Business School professor, and his co-authors posed the question, "How will you measure your life?"[5] The authors discussed success in work, relationships, and living a life of integrity. Christensen wrote, "If you take the time to figure out your purpose in life, I promise that you will look back on it as the most important thing you have ever learned."[6] The sixteenth-century French writer, Michel de Montaigne, wrote, "The great and glorious masterpiece of man is to live with purpose."[7]

People around you in the workplace will vary in how a sense of purpose affects their lives. Some people have lives of purpose but cannot articulate that purpose. Others struggle with determining their purpose. A few will know exactly what their lives are about. But many just live their lives as they unfold without thinking about purpose and possibilities—or goals.

Key: Setting goals at work and in life increases the odds of success.

We understand a lot about setting goals. We know how to do it; we have decades of research studying what works.[8] In a nutshell, goals must be specific. The goal, "I want to lose weight" is not specific; "I want to lose 20 pounds in the next six months" is specific—it also is measurable. You can step on the scales and chart your progress. In six months you will know if you are successful. From my experience, 20 pounds in six months is challenging, somewhat difficult but attainable. Specific, measurable, somewhat difficult—these are characteristics of goals that are most likely to motivate action.

Bruce returned to his office after the meeting of the supervisors with their director, Mr. Horn.

"So what's the latest, boss?" asked Mary Kay, a great worker and Bruce's right
hand.

"Horn wants us to increase our productivity."

"How much?"

"He didn't say."

"By when?"

"He didn't say."

"Did he give you any specifics?"

"Nope. Just said do our best."

Vague goal; no metrics; ambiguous information. What are the goals of
your organization? What are the goals for your workplace? Your work
group or team? Hopefully, they meet the requirements for good goals, but
sometimes they might not. If you work in an environment with clear, measurable, challenging goals, then there is a higher probability of accomplishing workplace goals and probably a higher level of commitment from
the employees.

Your coworkers probably vary widely in terms of personal goal setting. I
believe goal setting can make a big difference in one's life, especially if you
set goals correctly (as discussed above). I know people who go through
life just responding to whatever happens, with no planning, no thinking
about priorities, and few goals, if any. That is their choice. Some people
prefer to live their lives that way and just let events unfold. As for me, I
love life-long learning. There's so much I'd like to learn that I have to set
priorities. Few things are more valuable than time.

I made my first list of life goals without really realizing how important
goal setting was. I was a senior at the United States Air Force Academy. I
was 21 and soon would be graduating. I was sitting in a classroom, and
that day's lecture did not capture my attention; instead I daydreamed—
thinking about my future, my desire for a doctorate in psychology, a marriage with the woman of my dreams, a family, economic security. I thought
about the next 5 years, 10, 15, 20, and made some notes. Those few
notes—those goals—were guideposts. I accomplished those goals—and
somewhere I still have that list.

As the years passed and I learned more about goal setting, I started
reviewing and revising my goals annually, usually on a summer afternoon
in a hammock in the shade of a tree. What was working? Where was I in
terms of achieving certain goals? What goals needed to be added? Which
needed to be modified? I organized my goals into categories: personal,
financial, and professional with subcategories. I found that reflecting on
my goals helped me understand myself, where I was in life, where I wanted
to go, what I wanted to achieve. Even failing to achieve goals was insightful.

My goals reflected what was important to me. In one of the courses I teach, I assign a goal-setting exercise. Feedback from my students has been that the goal-setting exercise is one of the most important course assignments of their college careers.

When you look at your goals, you probably are looking at what you want to be your priorities. You might see in your goals your dominant life theme. They could reflect how you come at the world, how you give meaning to the world.

When I encountered Joseph Rychlak in a graduate course at Purdue University many years ago, I found a kindred soul. I had grown out of synch with the materialistic, reductionist view of the human being that prevails in most American psychology. At the core of scientific psychology is a hard determinism. What this means is that if we knew everything possible about a person—the smallest detail and genetics—then we should be able to totally predict that person's behavior, and even that person's choices. Of course, we cannot gather that much information so we can't make such predictions, but if we did have it then we could. In short, there is no free will—there is only the illusion of free will.

Rychlak disagreed. He wrote extensively about free will and offered a humanistic perspective of the individual.[9] He described the view of the human being in modern psychology as being derived primarily from the seventeenth-century philosopher, John Locke. People are born "tabula rasa," blank slates; experiences write on these blank slates. Locke's tabula rasa, however, is not the only view of the human being. Immanuel Kant, an eighteenth-century philosopher, held that people are "pro forma," we construct reality from our sensory inputs. We don't just process what is as it is; we have to convert our sensory inputs into perceptions. We perceive the world external to us, and in the perceiving we filter and construct. We give meaning to our experiences. In so doing, we make choices about the meanings we give our experiences; the meaning is not hardwired. It is in giving meaning to our experiences, in choosing how we will interpret our world, that we demonstrate our free will.[10] Because we can think dialectically, we can affirm meanings different from the meaning one might expect just from looking at our situation. If given "A," we can choose to affirm "not-A," an opposite point of view. We are indeed free. As the fictional Albus Dumbledore once told Harry Potter, "It is our choices, Harry, that show what we truly are, far more than our abilities."[11]

Rychlak embraced the Kantian perspective. He was hard-nosed in his use of the scientific method, but he developed a humanistic theory to test his hypotheses about people.[12] We construct our reality from the world around us, giving meaning to our world and our work. Consciously or subconsciously, we choose how we interpret our experience, what it means to us, and how we act based on the meaning we give it. The implications of this Rychlakean perspective are both practical and profound.

> **Key: To truly understand others, try to see the world through their eyes.**

To see how a person comes at the world and interprets situations, we have to think about that person introspectively.[13] We have to try to look through that person's eyes, to listen with that person's ears; this can be difficult. We live in our skin with all the perceptions we create. To stop and focus on another, to listen actively, to understand another person is hard to do. Having been married many years, I know. I am still working on this one. But trying to do this, no matter how incomplete the effort, will bring you closer to understanding another than if you do not try.

You will find that many of the people you encounter are not good listeners. They think they are but they are not. They do not listen to others for content and affect.

Erica enters Marcus's office, Marcus is sitting at his desk with the door to his right. "Have a seat," he says with a glance at Erica, "What can I do for you?" Marcus continues to type on his computer.

"If this is a good time, I'd like to give you a short update on the Wellington project." Erica says.
"Sure. Go ahead." Marcus says.
"I've got a summary if you'd like to look it over so we can discuss."
Marcus continues typing. "Keep talking. I'm listening." Marcus continues to type, still not looking at Erica.
Erica starts giving her update. The phone rings and Marcus answers, "Yeah, that works for me. Talk with you later. Bye."
After a short pause, Erica continues her report. Marcus nods occasionally.
"Well, that's all I have, Marcus. Any questions?" Erica asks.
"Nope, none right now. If I have any, I'll get back with you." Marcus turns to Erica, "Thanks much."
Erica leaves.

Contrary to popular thinking, you really cannot attend to two or more things at once and do them equally well. Attention might shift back and forth, but something has to give. Marcus made no effort to actively listen to Erica. He did not face her. He had no idea of her body language. He asked no questions to clarify points; he offered no paraphrased comments to show that he was really listening and that he understood. Marcus worked on whatever he was typing and answered a phone call. He might as well have told Erica to leave the report and not waste her time.

You cannot actively listen to every conversation. Active listening is very difficult to do.[14] But the key is to actively listen when the conversation is important, if not for you, then for the person speaking. Being an active listener is a skill that comes with practice. It is not natural for us to really listen well. How often when someone is talking with you are you formulating your reply in your mind? You aren't listening if you are formulating your response. Active listening is a skill worth developing. You will see and hear things that others miss.

> **Key: We are never totally bound by our environment; we have choices, limited as they might seem at times.**

One of the implications of Rychlakean theory is that we are never totally bound by our environment.[15] In the horrors of the concentration camp at Auschwitz, Viktor Frankl experienced wonder and great beauty in a magnificent sunset. There is free will; we always have choice. Even when our situation seems overwhelming, even when everything seems to be in our way or against us, there is choice.

The woman was in her 40s, a former student. She dropped by my office one afternoon without an appointment. I invited her to sit and we exchanged small talk. Then she came to the point of her visit.

> Dr. B, you probably don't remember me. I was in one of your management classes five years ago. I just wanted you to know that something you said changed my life. You were talking about how we were never totally bound by our situation, that we have choice. I really thought about that for several weeks. I realized you were right. At that time I was in a very abusive relationship. I saw no way out. I had lost hope. But the more I thought about it, the more I realized that you were right. I did have a choice. So I got help from some wonderful people. I got out of that relationship, Dr. B. Today I am happily married to a wonderful man. I just wanted you to know and to say thank you.

We talked for a few minutes and then she was gone. I barely remembered her. I had no idea of the hell she had been enduring when she was my student. We often do not really know another's situation, and you never know where a comment might lead.

Sometimes it is difficult to see that we have a choice. So often we attribute our responses to others, and not to ourselves. Consider this hypothetical story that I sometimes use in one of my courses.

My wife works through the day in her position as an educator. I work at home as a house husband. Every day I do household duties and prepare our evening meal. One day I decide to cook one of my fabulous Indonesian meals and I labor in the kitchen for hours. Finally, at around 5 p.m., my wife comes in the door after a hard day's work.

"Hi, what's for dinner?" she says with a smile.

To which I reply, "You know—it is the same thing every night. I work hard fixing dinner and you come home and the first thing you ask is, 'What's for dinner?' You never say, 'Hi, hunk, how was your day?'"

Increasingly upset, I talk louder and faster until I am screaming. "What's for dinner? What's for DINNER?! WHAT'S FOR DINNER!! YOU MAKE ME SO MAD!!"

Who made me mad? Ultimately, only you can make yourself mad. You have the choice how you respond, although it might not feel like you have a choice. Given a person who upsets us, we can choose to not let that person upset us. I did not say it was easy, but it can be done.

Key: Sometimes people just behave arbitrarily.

Another implication of Rychlakean theory is that people can behave arbitrarily without any reason other than they choose to do so. In these cases it is hard to see through another's eyes. A manager might use every motivational technique the manager knows, use every reinforcement available, and still not attain the desired response from an employee. Some people are just not going to respond as you would expect. As a manager I found this Rychlakean perspective to be helpful. I just had to deal with the results and do what was best for my organization.

You cannot really change anyone. You can make contingencies good— or bad—such that people are more likely to choose certain options. But, ultimately, people change when they choose to change. For example, research shows that people who experience health crises are more likely to make changes that result in healthy behaviors.

Nora was a young woman in love.

"Momma, I know you don't like Andy. I get it. He does drink a little too much sometimes. I know he has trouble holding a job. But, Momma, I love him. He makes me feel so . . . so . . . you know. He's really a great guy. I'll change him after we are married. I know I will."

Only if he chooses to change.

As you seek to understand those around you, seek to understand yourself. What are your goals? What is your purpose? What is most important to you? What is your motto? Covey suggested writing a personal mission statement. Doing so can help clarify your values and your direction in life. Ultimately, the question to be answered is that asked by Clayton Christensen and his co-authors: How will you measure your life?

Decoding the Workplace: Concluding Thoughts

The end of the semester always is a tough time in the academic year, obviously for students as they cram for final exams and complete papers and projects, but also for professors and instructors who lead the courses. I always find that there is so much more that I want the class to explore, more insights I want them to develop. It is the same with this book.

The fields of management and organizational behavior are vast. I never intended this book to be comprehensive. I have focused on concepts and ideas that I have found can really make a difference in the work lives of people. Some keys provide new understandings or perhaps different ways of viewing something about which you were not sure. Other keys might seem straightforward, even commonsensical. You might have thought, "Yeah, I know that," but when you went beyond the key to the discussion and examples, in some cases your understanding deepened. You might have had a thought, an insight, that you knew could help you with a situation or a decision. This happens every semester in my courses.

Most of my students also work. Some are working their way through college, others have been in the workplace for many years but never finished that degree, and still others are pursuing a graduate degree. Unsolicited, they tell me how concepts in our courses helped them in the workplace—to understand a situation, a coworker, a manager, or themselves. To solve a problem, find new opportunities, improve their effectiveness, and to earn promotions. My hope is that somewhere in this book you found at least one idea that made reading it worthwhile.

Decoding the workplace is never perfect. At times events will unfold around you about which you will not have a clue. Many times it will be the informal organization at play. But you will know more about what is happening because you will see the concepts and ideas about which you have read in this book—ideas and concepts that others might not see. Your understanding of workplace dynamics will be greater, and this will help you navigate organizational waters.

Steve had been in the workplace for several years and had been promoted twice. But Steve knew he could be more effective. He sought my help. We talked about understanding informal systems, the ways in which one builds personal power, the importance of active listening, the importance of managing one's impressions, and other concepts discussed in this book. With a little coaching, Steve developed a better ability to decode the workplace. He became even more effective.

One day Steve was at a meeting with people from other functions in his organization. The Chief Operating Officer attended and noticed Steve's performance. Afterward the COO talked with Steve, "Nice job in the meeting today. You really seemed to have things under control and made things happen in there. Haven't quite seen you like this before. Nice work."

Steve thanked the COO and then thought to himself, "I have learned so much. All these years in the workplace and I had never really understood what was happening around me." My guess is that, like Steve, no matter how long you have been in the workplace, there is something herein that was helpful.

There is no denying that, as individuals, we each are different. We extend different meanings to our worlds; we are motivated by different intrinsic and extrinsic rewards. To understand another person, we must think about that person introspectively as imperfect as that can be. But we have discussed many concepts that can help you understand people in situations and in organizations, such as norms, roles, groups, teams, organization socialization, and organization culture. With the keys as guidelines, you can make and test your own hypotheses about what is happening around you. Reflecting on your experiences should give you insights that can up your game.

I have tried to share findings and theories in a way that you would find useful. The knowledge gap between practitioners of management and scholars of management is too broad.[1] We need more and better plain-English translations of our research. We need more and better applications of what we have learned. I have tried through this book to move in that direction, to narrow the gap ever so slightly, to share concepts and ideas in a way that is both informative and interesting, to illustrate applications that can make a positive difference in your workplace.

Time is precious. If you have taken the time to read this far, I am honored. My intent was in some small way to help you better understand the workplace around you, better understand others, better understand yourself, to give you ideas to improve your effectiveness, and to give you ideas to improve your decision making. I hope you found something that can make your life in the workplace a little better. You have the keys.

Acknowledgments

The development of this book has been a journey. I undertook this journey because my students, many of whom were in the workplace, convinced me these ideas and stories needed to be shared with a wider audience. I am thankful to all my students, past and present, from whom I learned and continue to learn so much.

Early on the journey, Tom Volpe offered good conversation and underscored the corporate world's need for such a book. Likewise, early on another friend and I exchanged many ideas about the workplace. I turned to this friend for second opinions and feedback on early chapter drafts.

Along the way, Kim Polizotto and Charles Kroncke were very encouraging, reminding me ever so often, "You have to write the book." Similarly, Mary Ann Edwards, Jeff Hillard, and Phyllis Polizotto were steadfastly encouraging, telling me, "You'll get this done." I also thank A. X. Venu for his support, keen insights, and for reviewing much of the manuscript.

Therese S. Kinal, Margie Miller, and Todd Randall read early versions of the completed manuscript, provided good feedback, and inspired me with their comments. I am especially indebted to Scott Calhoun for detailed constructive criticism that made me a better writer and for great conversations that made the journey more enjoyable.

In the summer of 2012, I attended the Antioch Writers' Workshop in Yellow Springs, Ohio. My learning at this writers' workshop was exponential. The Antioch Writers' Workshop was a very significant milestone on this journey. In the fall of 2012 Mount St. Joseph University awarded me a sabbatical for one semester to complete the first draft of this book. I am grateful to the Antioch Writers' Workshop and Mount St. Joseph University for these opportunities.

Maryann Karinch of The Rudy Agency is a top agent for writers of non-fiction books on business topics. I feel extremely fortunate that she chose to represent me and work with me. Likewise, Hilary Claggett is one of the top acquisition editors in business nonfiction. I have been honored to work with her and the Praeger team.

This journey would not have been possible without the love and support of Emily, my partner in life. Without her this undertaking would have been too arduous. And to our son Jay and our daughter Kathy, thanks for keeping the faith.

My thanks to all acknowledged here, and to others who believed in me and believed in this book.

Notes

Preface

1. Stephen P. Robbins, *The Truth about Managing People . . . and Nothing but the Truth* (Upper Saddle River, NJ: Prentice Hall, 2002), xiv.

2. Douglas McGregor, *The Human Side of Enterprise* (New York: McGraw-Hill, 1960), 36.

Chapter 1

1. Jerald Greenberg, *Managing Behavior in Organizations*, 6th ed. (Upper Saddle River, NJ: Prentice Hall, 2012). Greenberg's book is representative of textbooks that review and summarize the field of organizational behavior, and are used in college and university courses.

Chapter 2

1. Ludwig von Bertalanffy, *General Systems Theory* (New York: Braziller, 1968).

2. Mark Davidson, *Uncommon Sense: The Life and Thought of Ludwig von Bertalanffy (1901–1972), Father of General Systems Theory* (Los Angeles: Tarcher, 1983), 25–26.

3. Madeline Drexler, "Our Bugs, Ourselves," *Harvard Public Health Magazine* (Spring 2013), http://www.hsph.harvard.edu/news/magazine/our-bugs -ourselves/.

4. Daniel Katz and Robert L. Kahn, *The Social Psychology of Organizations*, 2nd ed. (New York: Wiley, 1978).

5. Robert L. Cross and Andrew Parker, *The Hidden Power of Social Networks: Understanding How Work Really Gets Done* (Boston: Harvard Business School Press, 2004).

6. Marvin R. Weisbord, "Organizational Diagnosis: Six Places to Look for Trouble with or without a Theory," *Group & Organizational Studies* 1, no. 4 (1976): 430–447.

7. Jeffrey Kluger, "Remembering Neil Armstrong, a Man of Profound Skill and Preternatural Calm," *Time* (August 25, 2012), http://science.time.com/2012/08/25 /remembering-neil-armstrong-a-man-of-profound-skill-and-preternatural-calm/.

Chapter 3

1. Fred Luthans, Richard M. Hodgetts, and Stuart A. Rosenkrantz, *Real Managers* (Cambridge, MA: Ballinger, 1988).

2. Mary Follett, "The Giving of Orders," in *Dynamic Administration: The Collected Papers of Mary Parker Follett*, ed. Henry C. Metcalf and Lyndall Urwick (New York: Harper & Row, 1941), 50.

3. Joseph Luft and Harrington Ingham, "The Johari Window: A Graphic Model of Interpersonal Awareness," in *Proceedings of the Western Training Laboratory in Group Development* (Los Angeles: UCLA Extension Office, 1955).

4. Henry David Thoreau, *The Thoughts of Thoreau*, ed. Edwin W. Teale (New York: Dodd, Mead, & Company, 1962), 1.

5. Erving Goffman, *The Presentation of Self in Everyday Life* (Garden City, NY: Anchor, 1959).

Chapter 4

1. H. Roy Kaplan, "Lottery Winners: The Myth and Reality," *Journal of Gambling Behavior* 3 (Fall 1987): 168–178. *See also* Richard D. Arvey, Itzhak Harpaz, and Hui Liao, "Work Centrality and Post-Award Work Behavior of Lottery Winners," *Journal of Psychology* 138, no. 5 (2004): 404–420.

2. Douglas McGregor, *The Human Side of Enterprise* (New York: McGraw-Hill, 1960), 36–44.

3. Abraham H. Maslow, *Motivation and Personality* (New York: Harper & Brothers, 1954).

4. Richard M. Steers, *Introduction to Organizational Behavior* (Santa Monica, CA: Goodyear, 1981).

5. Frederick Herzberg, "One More Time: How Do You Motivate Employees," *Harvard Business Review* 46, no. 1 (1968): 53–62.

6. Nathan King, "Clarification and Evaluation of the Two-Factor Theory of Job Satisfaction," *Psychological Bulletin* 74, no. 1 (1970): 18–31.

7. J. Stacy Adams, "Toward an Understanding of Inequity," *Journal of Abnormal and Social Psychology* 67 (1963): 422–436. *See also* J. Stacy Adams, "Inequity in Social Exchange," in *Advances in Experimental Social Psychology*, vol. 2, ed. Leonard Berkowitz (New York: Academic Press, 1965), 267–299.

8. Leon Festinger, "A Theory of Social Comparison Processes," *Human Relations* 7 (1954): 117–140.

9. Victor H. Vroom, *Work and Motivation* (New York: Wiley, 1964).

10. Victor Vroom, *Then and Now: A Talk with Questions and Answers*, presented at Annual Meeting of the Academy of Management, Boston, MA, August 3–7, 2012.

Chapter 5

1. J. Richard Hackman, "Group Influences on Individuals," in *Handbook of Industrial and Organizational Psychology*, ed. Marvin D. Dunnette (Chicago: Rand McNally, 1976), 1495–1506.

2. Ibid., 1496.

3. Sheryl Sandberg, *Lean In: Women, Work, and the Will to Lead* (New York: Alfred A. Knopf, 2013), 5.

4. John A. Ballard and Jane A. Farrell, *Group Performance and Sex of the Leader: A Meta-Analysis*, presented at Annual Meeting of the American Psychological Association, New Orleans, LA, August 11–15, 1989.

5. David Benjamin Oppenheimer, "Exacerbating the Exasperating: Title VII Liability of Employers for Sexual Harassment Comitted [*sic*] by Their Supervisors," *Cornell Law Review* 81, no. 66 (1995): 91, http://scholarship.law.berkeley.edu/facpubs/1580.

6. Daniel C. Feldman, "The Development and Enforcement of Group Norms," *Academy of Management Review* 9, no. 1 (1984): 47–53.

7. Edwin P. Hollander, "Conformity, Status, and Idiosyncrasy Credit," *Psychological Review* 65, no. 2 (1958): 117–127.

Chapter 6

1. Robert K. Merton, *Social Theory and Social Structure*, rev. ed. (New York: Free Press, 1957).

2. Daniel Katz and Robert L. Kahn, *The Social Psychology of Organizations*, 2nd ed. (New York: Wiley, 1978), 194–195.

3. Virginia Ellen Schein, "The Relationship between Sex Role Stereotypes and Requisite Management Characteristics among Female Managers," *Journal of Applied Psychology* 60, no. 3 (1975): 340–344. *See also* Virginia Schein, "Sex Role Stereotyping, Ability, and Performance: Prior Research and Directions," *Personnel Psychology*, 31 (1978): 259–268. Given the changing role of women in the workplace, in 1989 Madeline Heilman and colleagues replicated Schein's 1973 study and obtained similar results. *See* Madeline E. Heilman, Caryn J. Block, Richard F. Martell, and Michael C. Simon, "Has Anything Changed? Current Characterizations of Men, Women, and Managers," *Journal of Applied Psychology* 74, no. 6 (1989): 935–942.

4. Jeffrey Pfeffer, *The Human Equation: Building Profits by Putting People First* (Boston: Harvard Business School Press, 1998), 149.

5. Mary Follett, "The Essentials of Leadership," in *Mary Parker Follett—Prophet of Management: A Celebration of Writings from the 1920s*, ed. Pauline Graham (Boston: Harvard Business School Press, 1995), 164. First published in *Freedom &*

Co-ordination: Lectures in Business Organisation, ed. Lyndall Urwich (London: Management Publications Trust, Ltd., 1949).

6. Gary N. Powell, D. Anthony Butterfield, and Jane D. Parent, "Gender and Managerial Stereotypes: Have the Times Changed?" *Journal of Management* 28, no. 2 (2002): 177.

7. Rosabeth Moss Kanter, *Men and Women of the Corporation* (New York: Basic Books, 1977).

8. Robert L. Kahn, Donald M. Wolfe, Robert P. Quinn, J. Diedrick Snoek, and Robert A. Rosenthal, *Organizational Stress: Studies in Role Conflict and Ambiguity* (New York: Wiley, 1964). This is the seminal work in which Kahn and colleagues identified and clarified the various types of role conflict discussed herein in Chapter 6.

9. George Graen, "Role-Making Processes within Complex Organizations," in *Handbook of Industrial and Organizational Psychology*, ed. Marvin D. Dunnette (Chicago: Rand McNally, 1976), 1238.

Chapter 7

1. Robert Rickover, "My Father Remembered," *Prairie Fire* (December 2008), http://prairiefirenewspaper.com/2008/12/my-father-remembered.

2. Gordan Runyan, *Prowl* (Los Alamos, NM: Deo Volente, 2000), 153.

3. Edgar H. Schein, "The Individual, the Organization, and the Career: A Conceptual Scheme," *Journal of Applied Behavioral Science* 7, no. 3 (1971): 401–426.

4. Helena D. Cooper-Thomas and Neil Anderson, "Organizational Socialization: A New Theoretical Model and Recommendations for Future Research and HRM Practices in Organizations," *Journal of Managerial Psychology* 21, no. 5 (2006): 492–516.

5. William H. Whyte, Jr., *The Organization Man* (New York: Simon and Schuster, 1956).

Chapter 8

1. Jon R. Katzenbach and Douglas K. Smith, "The Discipline of Teams," *Harvard Business Review* 69, no. 2 (1991): 111–120.

2. Natalie J. Allen and Tracy D. Hecht, "The 'Romance of Teams': Toward an Understanding of Its Psychological Underpinnings and Implications," *Journal of Occupational and Organizational Psychology* 77 (2004): 439, 444.

3. David A. Nadler and Michael L. Tushman, *Competing by Design: The Power of Organizational Architecture* (New York: Oxford University Press, 1998), 13.

4. Ibid., 11.

5. Richard L. Daft, *Organization Theory & Design,* 11th ed. (Mason, OH: South-Western, 2013), 99–107.

6. Stephen P. Robbins, *Organization Theory: Structures, Designs, and Applications,* 3rd ed. (Englewood Cliffs, NJ: Prentice-Hall, 1990).

7. Japan Echo Inc., "The McDonald's Effect: Fast-Food Giant Triggers a Price-Cutting Wave," *Japan Information Network* (August 21, 2001), http://web-japan.org/trends01/article/010820bus_r.html. *See also* George Ritzer, *The McDonaldization of Society,* 6th ed. (Thousand Oaks, CA: Sage, 2010).

8. David A. Nadler and Michael L. Tushman, *Competing by Design: The Power of Organizational Architecture* (New York: Oxford University Press, 1998). Richard L. Daft, *Organization Theory & Design,* 11th ed. (Mason, OH: South-Western, 2013). These are good sources for learning about factors that affect organization design.

9. Rob Cross and Andrew Parker, *The Hidden Power of Social Networks: Understanding How Work Really Gets Done in Organizations* (Boston, MA: Harvard Business School Press, 2004). *See also* Rob Cross, Nitin Nohria, and Andrew Parker, "Six Myths about Informal Networks—and How to Overcome Them," *MIT Sloan Management Review* 43, no. 3 (2002): 67–75.

10. Kenneth E. Olive and John A. Ballard, "Changes in Employee Smoking Behaviors Following Implementation of Restrictive Smoking Policies," *Southern Medical Journal* 89, no. 7 (1996): 699–706. *See also* Kenneth E. Olive and John A. Ballard, "Attitudes of Patients Toward Smoking by Health Professionals," *Public Health Reports* 107, no. 3 (1992): 335–339.

Chapter 9

1. *Working Time in the Twenty-First Century: Report for Discussion at the Tripartite Meeting of Experts on Working-Time Arrangements (17–21 October 2011)* (Geneva: International Labour Office, 2011), 26, http://www.ilo.org/wcmsp5/groups/public/—ed_protect/—protrav/—travail/documents/publication/wcms_161734.pdf.

2. Thomas L. Friedman, *The Lexus and the Olive Tree: Understanding Globalization* (New York: Farrar, Straus, and Giroux, 1999).

3. Edgar H. Schein, *Organizational Culture and Leadership,* 4th ed. (San Francisco: Jossey-Bass, 2010).

4. William H. Rodgers, *Think: A Biography of the Watsons and IBM* (New York: Stein and Day, 1969). *See also* Craig E. Johnson, *Organizational Ethics: A Practical Approach,* 2nd ed. (Thousand Oaks, CA: Sage, 2011).

5. Alyssa Roenigk, "An Unforgettable Sunday Afternoon for Lauren Hill," espnW, (November 5, 2014), http://espn.go.com/espnw/news-commentary/article/11811314/an-unforgettable-sunday-afternoon-lauren-hill.

6. Thomas H. Davenport, "The Fad That Forgot People," *Fast Company* (November 1995), http://www.fastcompany.com/26310/fad-forgot-people.

Chapter 10

1. John P. Kotter, *John P. Kotter on What Leaders Really Do* (Boston: Harvard Business School Press, 1999), 10–11.

2. John A. Ballard and Nancy Waldeck, "The Leadership Mess: Toward a More Inspirational Approach," presented at the Annual Meeting of the Association for Politics and the Life Sciences, Cincinnati, OH, October 13–15, 2011.

3. Richard H. Hughes, Robert C. Ginnett, and Gordon J. Murphy, *Leadership: Enhancing the Lessons of Experience,* 7th ed. (New York: McGraw-Hill/Irwin, 2012), 5.

4. Stephen J. Zaccaro and Richard J. Klimoski, "The Nature of Organizational Leadership: An Introduction," in *The Nature of Organizational Leadership: Understanding the Performance Imperatives Confronting Today's Leaders,* ed. Stephen J. Zaccaro and Richard J. Klimoski (San Francisco: Jossey-Bass, 2001), 5.

5. J. Richard Hackman and Ruth Wageman, "Asking the Right Questions about Leadership: Discussion and Conclusions," *American Psychologist* 62, no. 1 (2007): 43.

6. Bernard Bass, and Ronald E. Riggio, *Transformational Leadership* (Mahwah, NJ: Lawrence Erlbaum, 2006).

7. Jeffrey Pfeffer, "The Ambiguity of Leadership," *Academy of Management Review* 2 (1977): 104–112.

8. James R. Meindl, "On Leadership: An Alternative to the Conventional Wisdom," in *Research in Organizational Behavior,* vol. 12, ed. Barry M. Staw and Larry L. Cummings (Greenwich, CT: JAI Press, 1990), 161.

9. Robert Hogan, Robert Raskin, and Dan Fazzini, "The Dark Side of Charisma," in *Measures of Leadership,* ed. Kenneth E. Clark and Miriam B. Clark (West Orange, NJ: Leadership Library of America, 1990), 343–354.

10. Launor F. Carter, "Some Research on Leadership in Small Groups," in *Groups, Leadership, and Men: Research in Human Relations,* ed. Harold Guetzkow (Pittsburgh, PA: Carnegie Press, 1951), 146–157.

11. Abraham Zaleznik, "Managers and Leaders: Are They Different?" *Harvard Business Review* (May-June 1977): 67–78.

12. David L. Cawthon, "Leadership: The Great Man Theory Revisited," *Business Horizons* (May-June 1996): 1.

13. Robert J. House and Mary L. Baetz, "Leadership: Some Empirical Generalizations and New Research Directions," in *Research in Organizational Behavior,* vol. 1, ed. Barry M. Staw (Greenwich, CT: JAI Press, 1979), 341–423.

14. The Rev. Fred Shuttlesworth, in-person conversation with the author (November 16, 2004).

15. Melinda Beck, "The Sleepless Elite," *The Wall Street Journal* (April 5, 2001), http://online.wsj.com/news/articles/SB10001424052748703712504576242701 752957910?mg=reno64-wsj.

16. David L. Cawthon, "Leadership: The Great Man Theory Revisited," *Business Horizons* (May-June 1996): 3.

17. Douglas McGregor, *The Human Side of Enterprise* (New York: McGraw-Hill, 1960), 33–44.

18. Ibid., 45–57.

19. Chester A. Schriesheim and Barbara J. Bird, "Contributions of the Ohio State Studies to the Field of Leadership," *Journal of Management* 5, no. 2 (1979): 135–145.

20. Fred E. Fiedler, *A Theory of Leadership Effectiveness* (New York: McGraw-Hill, 1967).

21. Robert J. House, "A Path-Goal Theory of Leader Effectiveness," *Administrative Science Quarterly* 16, no. 3 (1971): 321–338. Martin G. Evans, "Extensions of a Path-Goal Theory of Motivation," *Journal of Applied Psychology* 59, no. 2 (1974): 172–178.

22. Mary Follett, "The Essentials of Leadership," in *Mary Parker Follett—Prophet of Management: A Celebration of Writings from the 1920s*, ed. Pauline Graham (Boston: Harvard Business School Press, 1995), 164. First published in *Freedom & Co-ordination: Lectures in Business Organisation*, ed. Lyndall Urwich (London: Management Publications Trust, Ltd., 1949), 170.

23. John J. Gabarro and John P. Kotter, "Managing Your Boss," *Harvard Business Review* (May-June 1993), 150–157.

24. Ibid., 152.

25. Wickham Skinner and W. Earl Sasser, "Managers with Impact: Versatile and Inconsistent," *Harvard Business Review* (November-December 1977): 147.

26. Peter F. Drucker, *Management Challenges for the 21st Century* (New York: Harper Business, 1999), 169.

27. John J. Gabarro and John P. Kotter, "Managing Your Boss," *Harvard Business Review* (May-June 1993): 152.

28. Mary Follett, "The Essentials of Leadership," in *Mary Parker Follett—Prophet of Management: A Celebration of Writings from the 1920s*, ed. Pauline Graham (Boston: Harvard Business School Press, 1995), 164. First published in *Freedom & Co-ordination: Lectures in Business Organisation*, ed. Lyndall Urwich (London: Management Publications Trust, Ltd., 1949), 172.

Chapter 11

1. John R. P. French, Jr., and Bertram Raven, "The Bases of Power," in *Studies in Social Power*, ed. Dorwin Cartwright (Ann Arbor, MI: Institute for Social Research, University of Michigan, 1959), 150–167.

2. John P. Kotter, "Power, Dependence, and Effective Management," *Harvard Business Review* (July-August 1977): 129–130.

3. Ibid., 130–131.

4. Rosabeth Moss Kanter, *Men and Women of the Corporation* (New York: Basic Books, 1977), 169.

5. Robert B. Cialdini, *Influence: Science and Practice*, 4th ed. (Boston: Allyn and Bacon, 2001), 150–152.

6. John P. Kotter, "Power, Dependence, and Effective Management," *Harvard Business Review* (July-August 1977): 131–132.

7. Philip B. Crosby, "The Management Challenge: Quality and Competitiveness," in John M. Ivancevich, Peter Lorenzi, and Steven J. Skinner, with Philip B. Crosby, *Management: Quality and Competitiveness*, 2nd ed. (New York: McGraw-Hill, 1997), 14.

Chapter 12

1. Rosabeth Moss Kanter, *Men and Women of the Corporation* (New York: Basic Books, 1977), 176–181.

2. John D. Breeze, "Harvest from the Archives: The Search for Fayol and Carlioz," *Journal of Management* 11, no. 1 (1985): 45.

3. Rosabeth Moss Kanter, *Men and Women of the Corporation* (New York: Basic Books, 1977), 181–186.

4. Ibid., 182.

5. John P. Kotter, "Power, Dependence, and Effective Management," *Harvard Business Review* (July-August 1977): 135–136.

6. Jeffrey Pfeffer, *Managing with Power: Politics and Influence in Organizations* (Boston: Harvard Business School Press, 1992).

7. Rosabeth Moss Kanter, *Men and Women of the Corporation* (New York: Basic Books, 1977), 186–189.

Chapter 13

1. Cynthia D. Fisher, "Why Do Lay People Believe That Satisfaction and Performance Are Correlated? Possible Sources of a Commonsense Theory," *Journal of Organizational Behavior* 24 (2003): 753–777.

2. Christian Dormann and Dieter Zapf, "Job Satisfaction: A Meta-Analysis of Stabilities," *Journal of Organizational Behavior* 22 (2001): 483.

3. Robert Hoppock, *Job Satisfaction* (New York: Harper and Brothers, 1935).

4. Gail Ghazzawi, "Job Satisfaction Antecedents and Consequences: A New Conceptual Framework and Research Agenda," *The Business Review, Cambridge* 11, no. 2 (2008): 1–10.

5. Martin Fishbein and Icek Ajzen, *Belief, Attitude, Intention, and Behavior: An Introduction to Theory and Research* (Reading, MA: Addison-Wesley, 1975).

6. Edwin A. Locke, "The Nature and Causes of Job Satisfaction," in *Handbook of Industrial and Organizational Psychology*, ed. Marvin D. Dunnette (Chicago: Rand McNally, 1976), 1319–1328. Locke's review is the basis for the job satisfaction discussion presented herein, unless otherwise referenced.

7. Adam M. Grant, "Leading with Meaning: Beneficiary Contact, Prosocial Impact, and the Performance Effect of Transformational Leadership," *Academy of Management Journal* 55, no. 2 (2012): 458–476.

8. Louis R. Pondy, "Organizational Conflict: Concept and Models," *Administrative Science Quarterly* 12, no. 2 (1967), 296–320.

9. Hans Selye, *The Stress of Life*, rev. ed. (New York: McGraw-Hill, 1976).

10. Joseph C. Rode, "Job Satisfaction and Life Satisfaction Revisited: A Longitudinal Test of an Integrated Model," *Human Relations* 57, no. 9 (2004): 1205–1230.

11. Erdman Palmore, "Predicting Longevity: A Follow-up Controlling for Age," *The Gerontologist* 9 (1969): 247–250.

Chapter 14

1. Viktor E. Frankl, *Man's Search for Meaning* (Boston: Beacon Press, 1959).

2. Ann Howard and Douglas W. Bray, *Managerial Lives in Transition: Advancing Age and Changing Times* (New York: Guilford Press, 1988).

3. Joseph F. Rychlak, *Personality and Life-Style of Young Male Managers: A Logical Learning Theory Analysis* (San Diego, CA: Academic Press, 1982).

4. Stephen Covey, *The 7 Habits of Highly Effective People* (New York: Fireside, 1989), 111.

5. Clayton M. Christensen, James Allworth, and Karen Dillon, *How Will You Measure Your Life?* (New York: HarperCollins, 2012).

6. Ibid., 205.

7. "Michel de Montaigne > Quotes," Goodreads (2014), http://www.goodreads .com/author/quotes/17241.Michel_de_Montaigne?page=3.

8. Edwin A. Locke and Gary P. Latham, "Building a Practically Useful Theory of Goal Setting and Task Motivation: A 35-Year Odyssey," *American Psychologist* 57, no. 9 (2002): 707–717.

9. Joseph F. Rychlak, *The Psychology of Rigorous Humanism,* 2nd ed. (New York: New York University Press, 1988).

10. Joseph F. Rychlak, *Discovering Free Will and Personal Responsibility* (New York: Oxford University Press, 1979).

11. J. K. Rowling, *Harry Potter and the Chamber of Secrets* (New York: Scholastic Press, 1998), 333.

12. Joseph F. Rychlak, *Logical Learning Theory: A Human Teleology and Its Empirical Support* (Lincoln, NE: University of Nebraska Press, 1994).

13. Joseph F. Rychlak, *Discovering Free Will and Personal Responsibility* (New York: Oxford University Press, 1979), 254–255.

14. Carl R. Rogers and Richard E. Farson, *Active Listening* (Chicago: Industrial Relations Center, The University of Chicago, 1957).

15. Joseph F. Rychlak, *Discovering Free Will and Personal Responsibility* (New York: Oxford University Press, 1979), 245.

Conclusion

1. Ramon J. Aldag, "Images of the Academy. Presidential Address to the Academy of Management," *Academy of Management News* 22, no. 4 (1992): 1–3.

Index

About the Author

John Ballard, PhD, is professor of management at Mount St. Joseph University in Cincinnati, Ohio. In 2013, *Cincy Magazine* honored him as one of Cincinnati's Outstanding Educators. A graduate of the United States Air Force Academy, during his years as an officer Dr. Ballard reinvented Air Force management consulting, and saved U.S. taxpayers millions of dollars.

Dr. Ballard earned degrees at the University of Southern Mississippi and Purdue University. He began his academic career at the Air Force Institute of Technology, the graduate school of the U.S. Air Force. He has served on the management faculty at Wittenberg University, Springfield, Ohio, and Miami University of Ohio, and taught as part of Central Michigan University's Global Campus. A management scholar with more than 50 papers and presentations, Dr. Ballard has received multiple awards and served on the editorial board of one of the most influential journals in management education, the *Academy of Management Learning & Education* journal. He shares practical implications of academic research through his blog, "Leadership, Management, and Life in the Workplace," at www.johnballardphd.com.

Dr. Ballard is married to Emily, his seventh grade sweetheart. He loves star gazing, U2, The Radiators from Space, Pollock's *Lavender Mist*, the plays of Tom Stoppard, and good Indonesian cuisine.